WAS GENGHIS KHAN REALLY MEAN?

Biography of Famous People | Children's Biography Books

Speedy Publishing LLC

40 E. Main St. #1156

Newark, DE 19711

www.speedypublishing.com

Copyright 2017

All Rights reserved. No part of this book may be reproduced or used in any way or form or by any means whether electronic or mechanical, this means that you cannot record or photocopy any material ideas or tips that are provided in this book

Genghis Khan was the Supreme Khan of the Mongols from 1206 until 1227. He was born in 1162 and died in 1227. He was most known for being the Founder of the Mongol Empire.

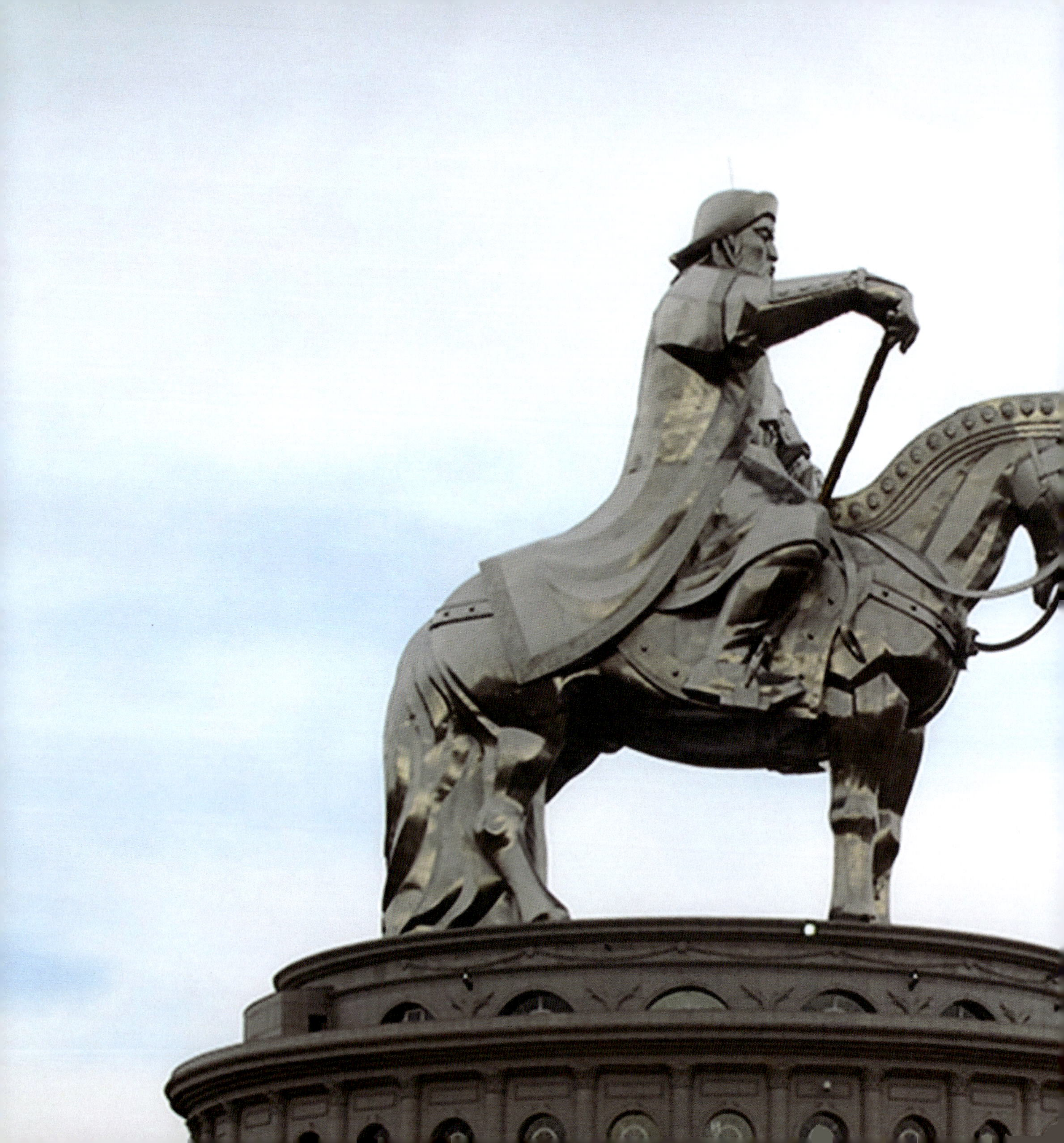

Read further to learn about his life and accomplishments, then you can decide if he really was a mean person.

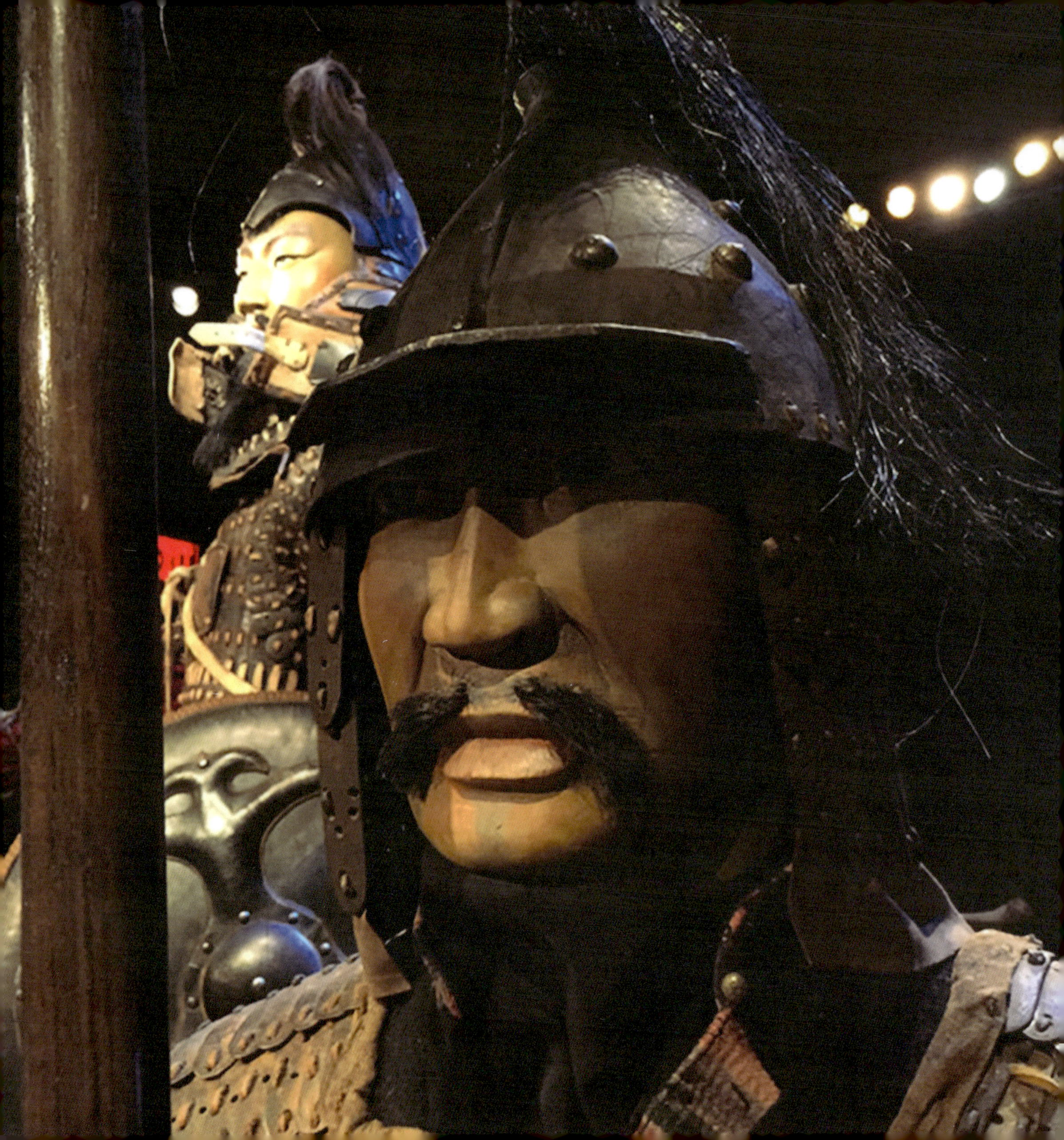

WHAT DID HE LOOK LIKE?

Not much is known about his personal life or his appearance, even though he was a very influential person. There are no surviving portraits or sculptures, and what information is available is unreliable or contradictory. He is mostly described as strong and tall, and having a flowy mane of hair with a bushy, long beard.

One of the more surprising descriptions comes from the 14th century chronicler Rashid al-Din, claiming that Genghis had green eyes and red hair. This account, however, is questionable since he had never met him. However, these features were known to be possible among the Mongols who were an ethnically diverse tribe.

Rashid-al-Din

Memorial of Genghis Khan

EARLY LIFE

Genghis was raised on the cold, harsh Mongolia plains. As a boy, he was known by the name Temujin, meaning "finest steel". Yesugai, his father, was the khan (chief) of the tribe. Temujin enjoyed his childhood, even though it was difficult. He liked to hunt with his brothers, and he also enjoyed riding horses.

Even as a child, he had to contend with the brutal life of the Mongolian Steppe. The rival Tatars had poisoned his father when he was nine, and he and his family then became expelled from their own tribe and his mother was left to raise her seven children by herself.

Mongolian Steppe

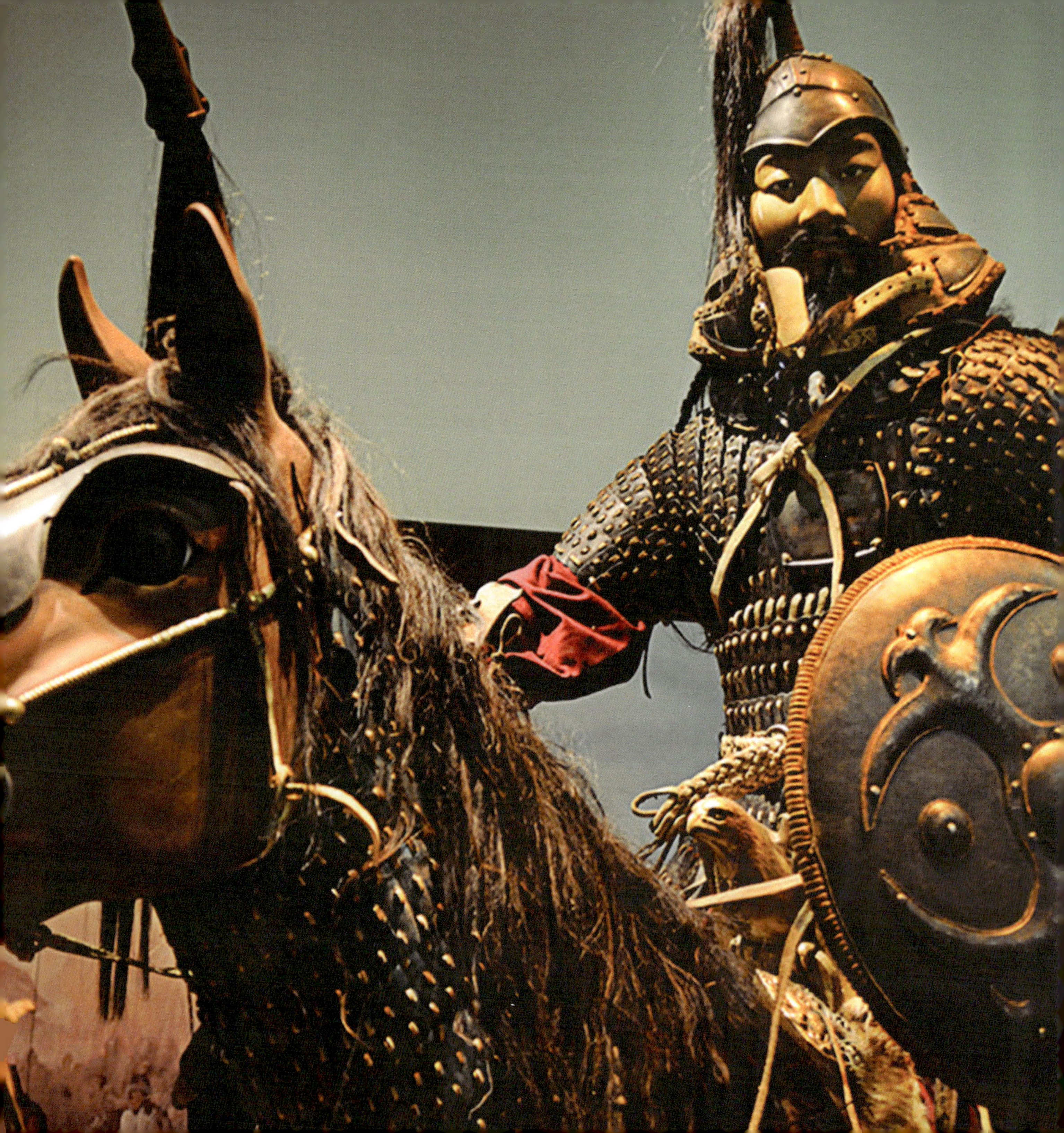

Genghis was raised foraging and hunting for survival, and as a child he may have killed his half-brother in a fight over food. As a teenager, he and his young wife were abducted by rival clans and he had to spend time in slavery prior to making an escape. In spite of these hardships, by his 20s he had demonstrated himself to be a formidable leader and warrior.

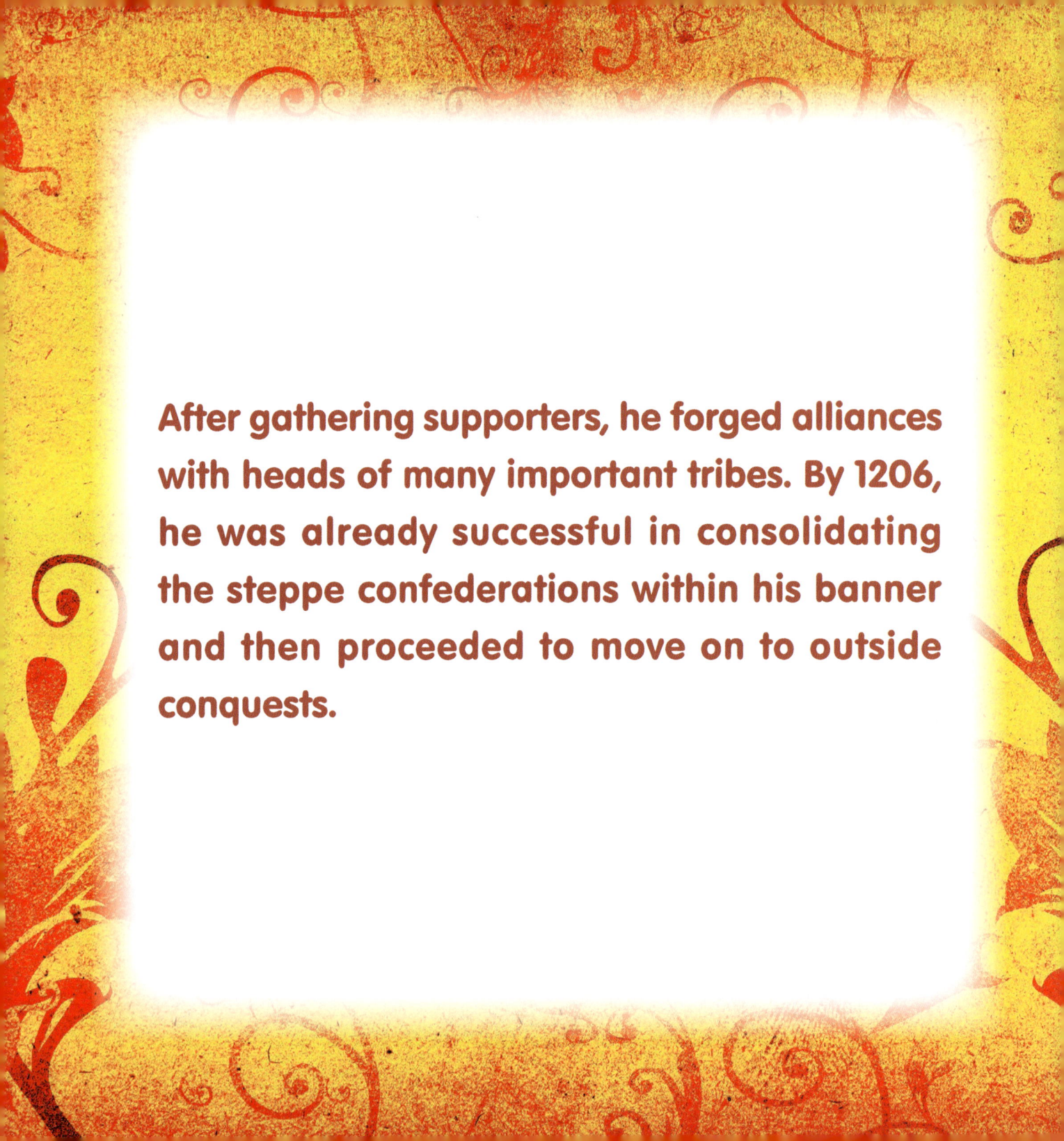

After gathering supporters, he forged alliances with heads of many important tribes. By 1206, he was already successful in consolidating the steppe confederations within his banner and then proceeded to move on to outside conquests.

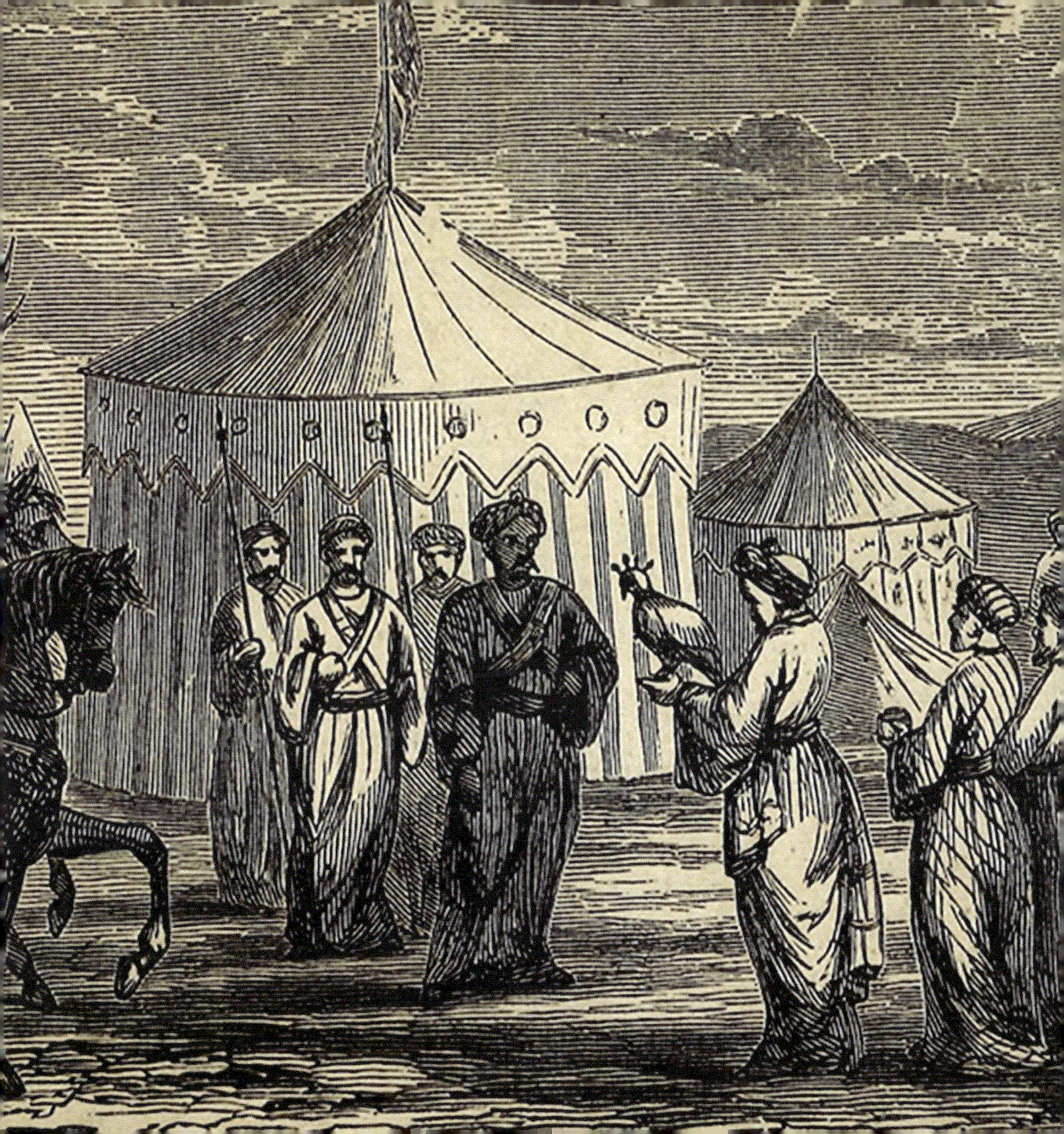

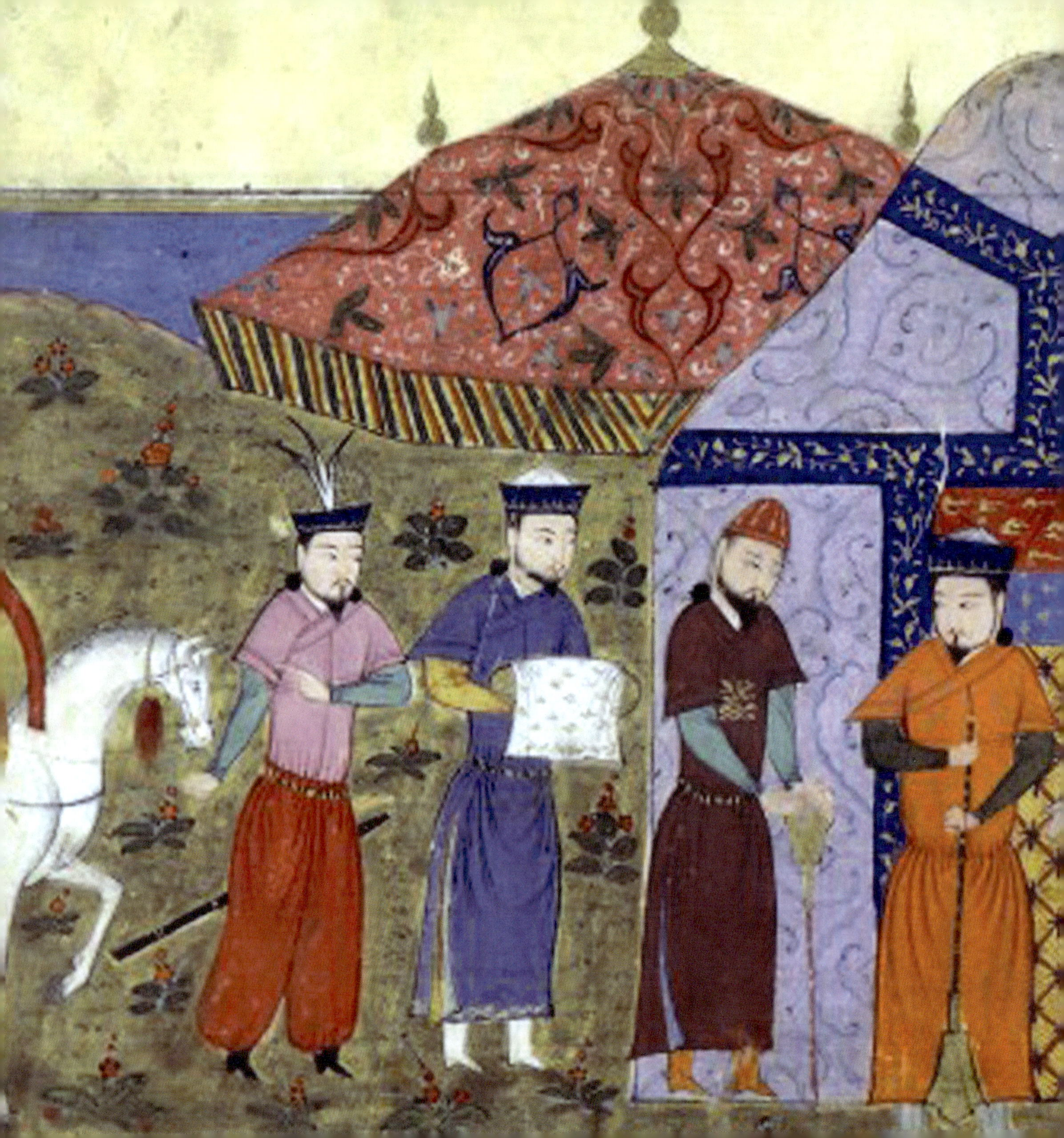

MARRIED

At the young age of nine, he was sent off to live with Borte, his future wife, and her tribe. After a few years had passed, he found out that his father was poisoned by the enemy Tartars, and returned home to become Khan of his home tribe.

BETRAYED

When Temujin returned home, he found that another warrior had betrayed his family, taking over the role of khan, and then proceeded to kick Temujin and his family out of the tribe. They were barely able to survive on their own, but he was not ready to give up. He and his family were able to survive the horrendous winter and he then began plotting revenge against the Tartars.

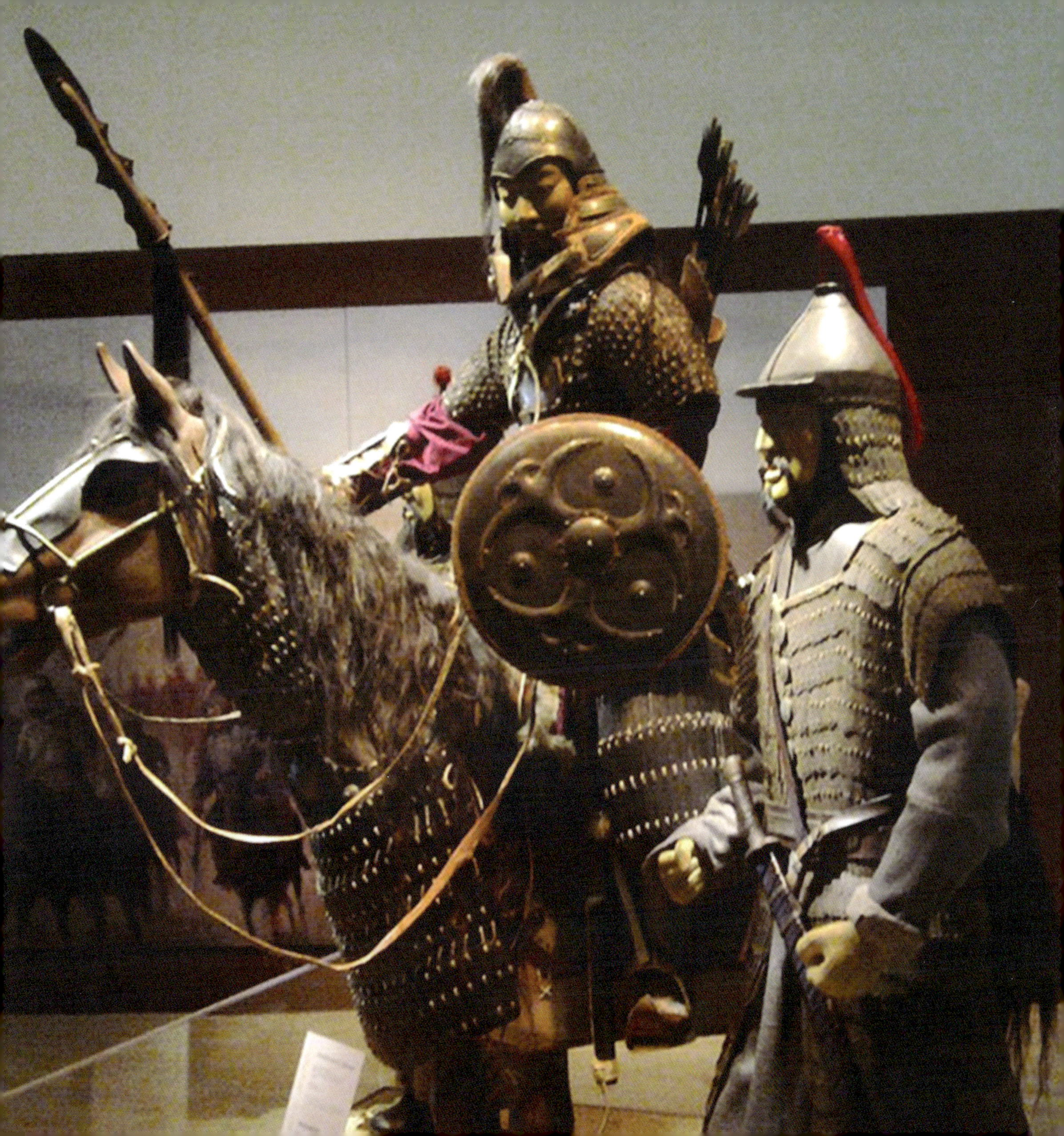

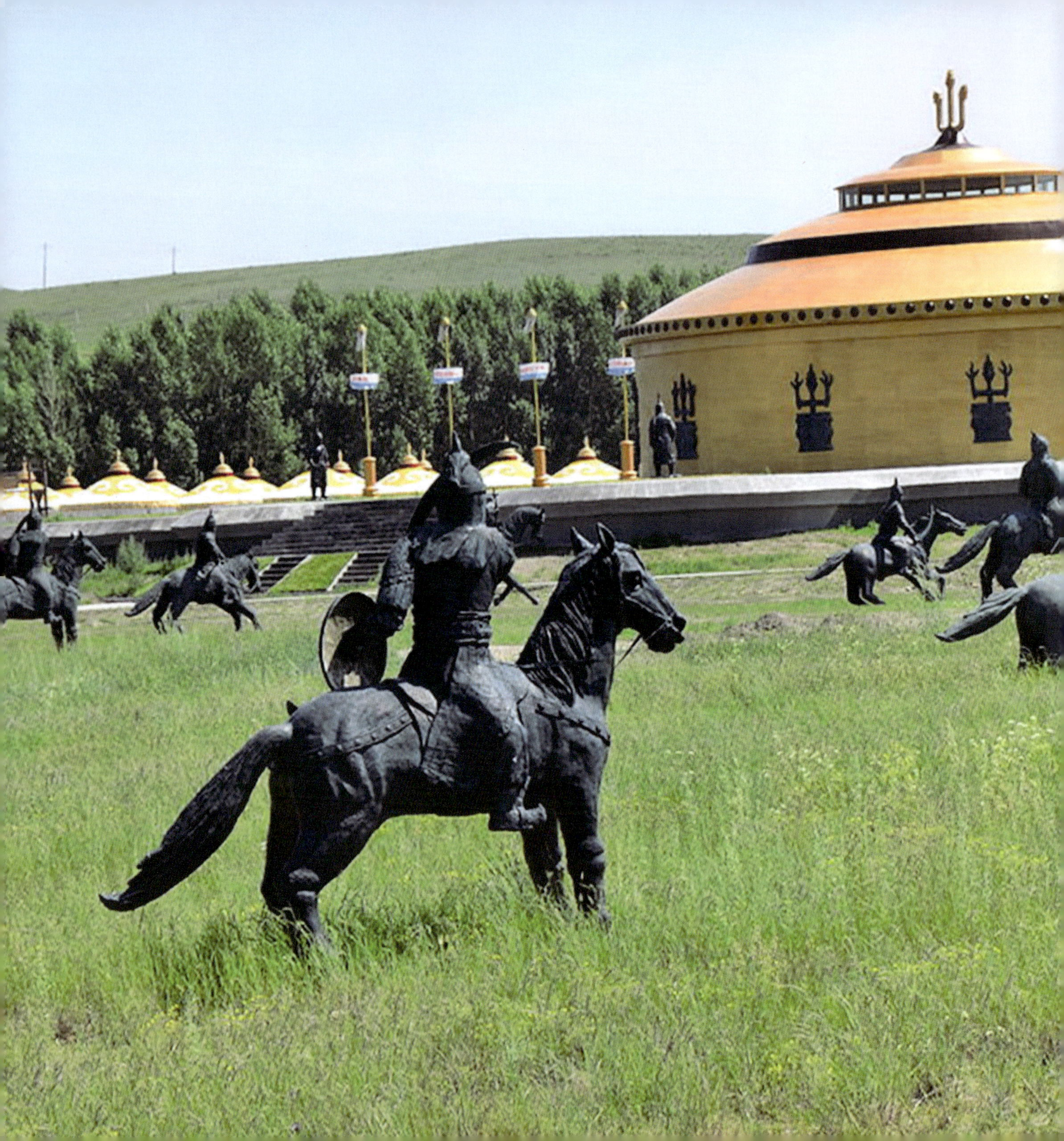

BUILDING AN ARMY

Temujin began building his own tribe during the next few years. He proceeded to marry Borte and became aligned with her tribe. He was known to be a brutal and fierce fighter, admired by the Mongols because of his courage. He continued to build his army of warriors until it was large enough, and forceful enough, to overtake the Tartars.

REVENGE ON THE TARTARS

Once he had fought the Tartars, he showed no remorse. He went on to decimate their army and killed their leaders. He began conquering the enemy Mongol tribes. He knew they needed unity. Once he had conquered his greatest enemy, the other Mongol tribes followed him. They called him Genghis Khan, meaning "ruler of all".

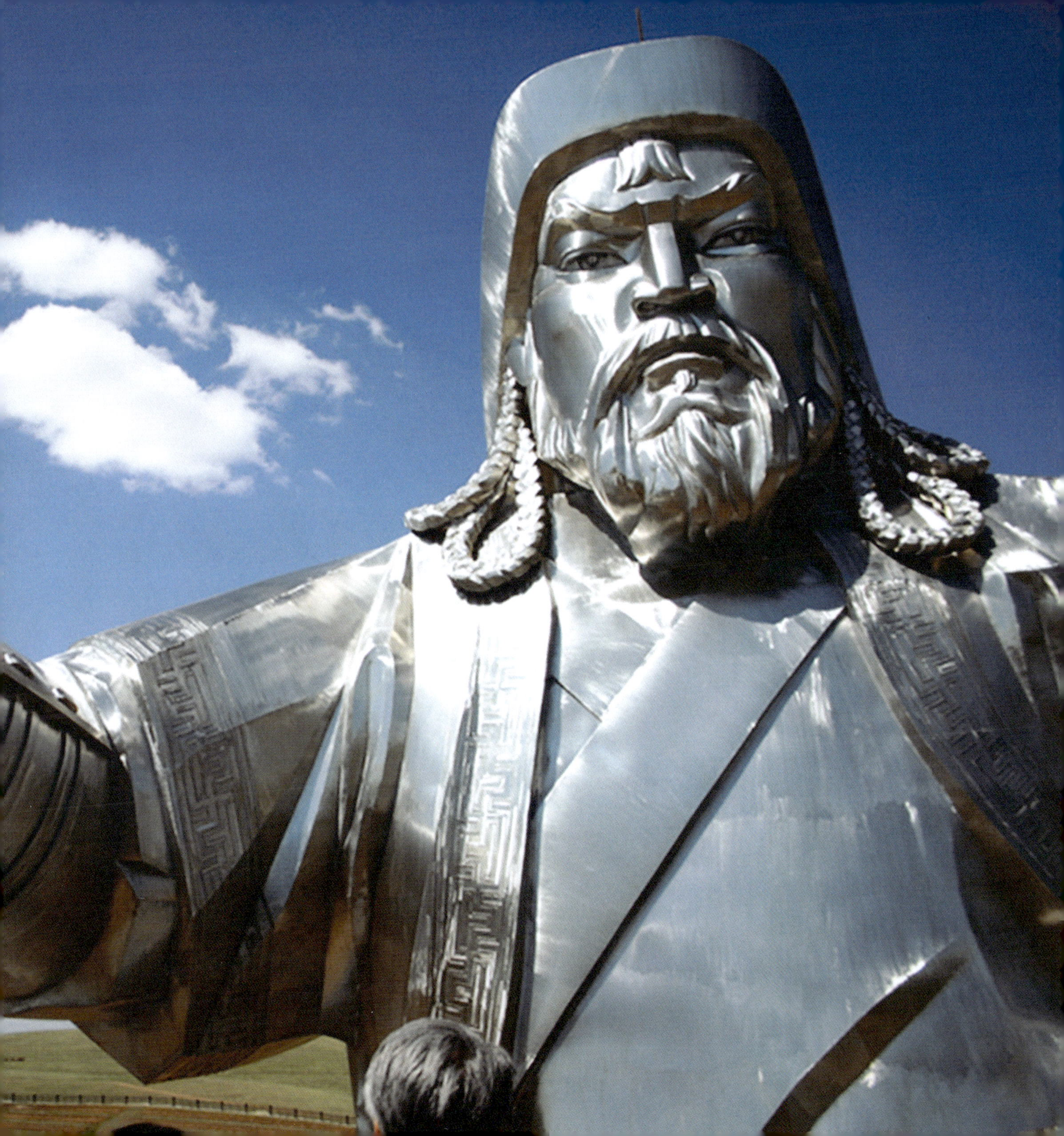

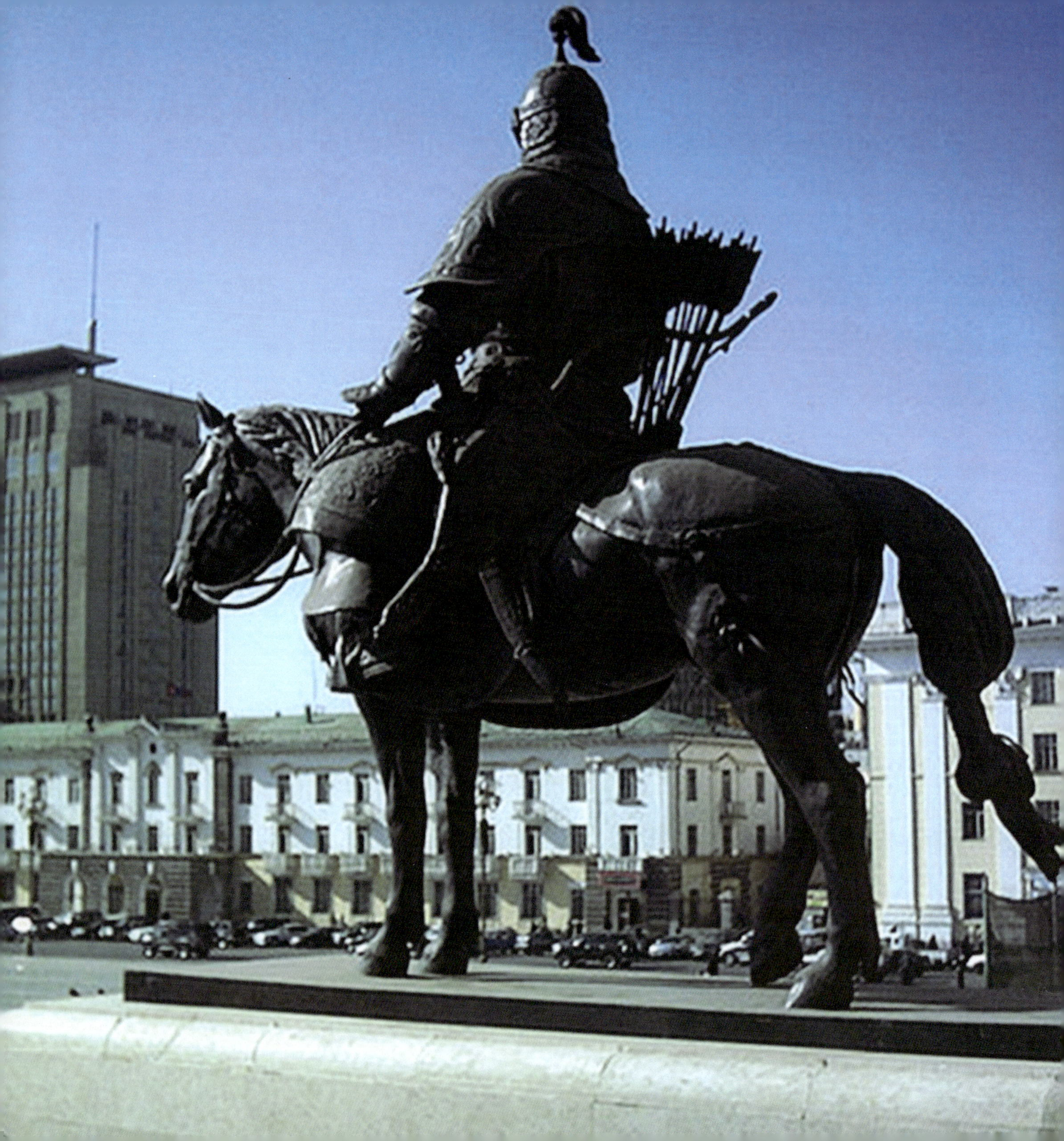

A BRILLIANT GENERAL

Genghis became a brilliant general. He called his soldiers "gurans" and organized them in groups of about 1000. They would train every day on battle tactics and would use smoke signals, drums, and flags for sending messages throughout his army quickly. They were well-armed and trained to ride horses and fight starting at a very young age.

They controlled their horses by only using their legs and would fire deadly arrows as they rode at full speed. He was also known to use innovative strategies on the battlefield. He would on occasion send in small forces and then have them retreat. Once their enemy charged back at the smaller force, they would find themselves surrounded by a pack of the Mongol warriors.

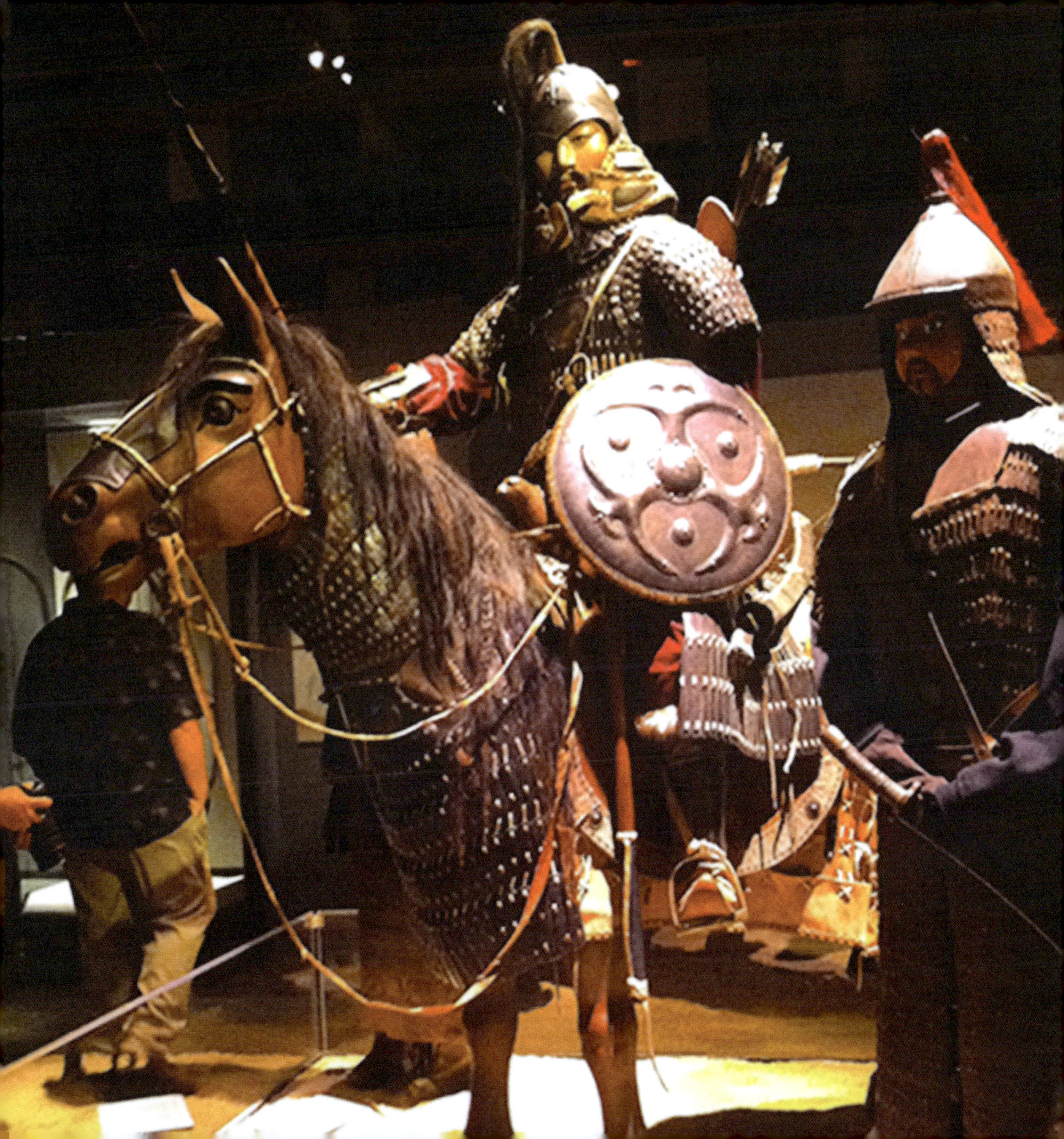

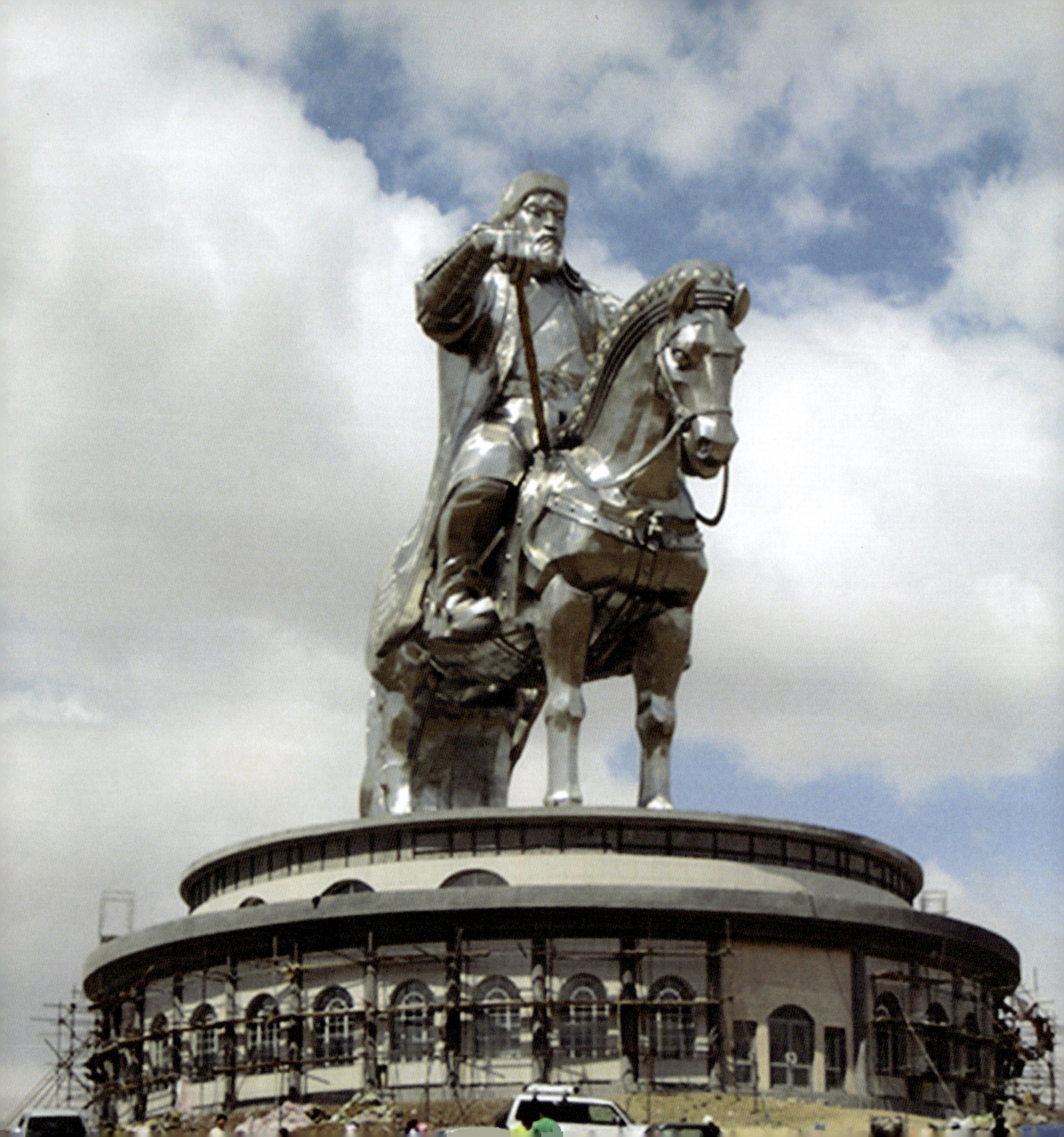

Jebe became one of his best generals. He had once been an enemy that shot Genghis during battle using an arrow. Genghis was impressed and spared Jefe's life. Jebe became known as "The Arrow".

LEADER

Genghis Khan was known to be a strong leader. He may have been cruel and lethal to the enemies, but he was loyal to those who believed in him. He launched a written code of law which came to be known as the Yasak. He would promote soldiers who performed well, regardless of their background. He expected his own sons to perform well if they desired to be leaders.

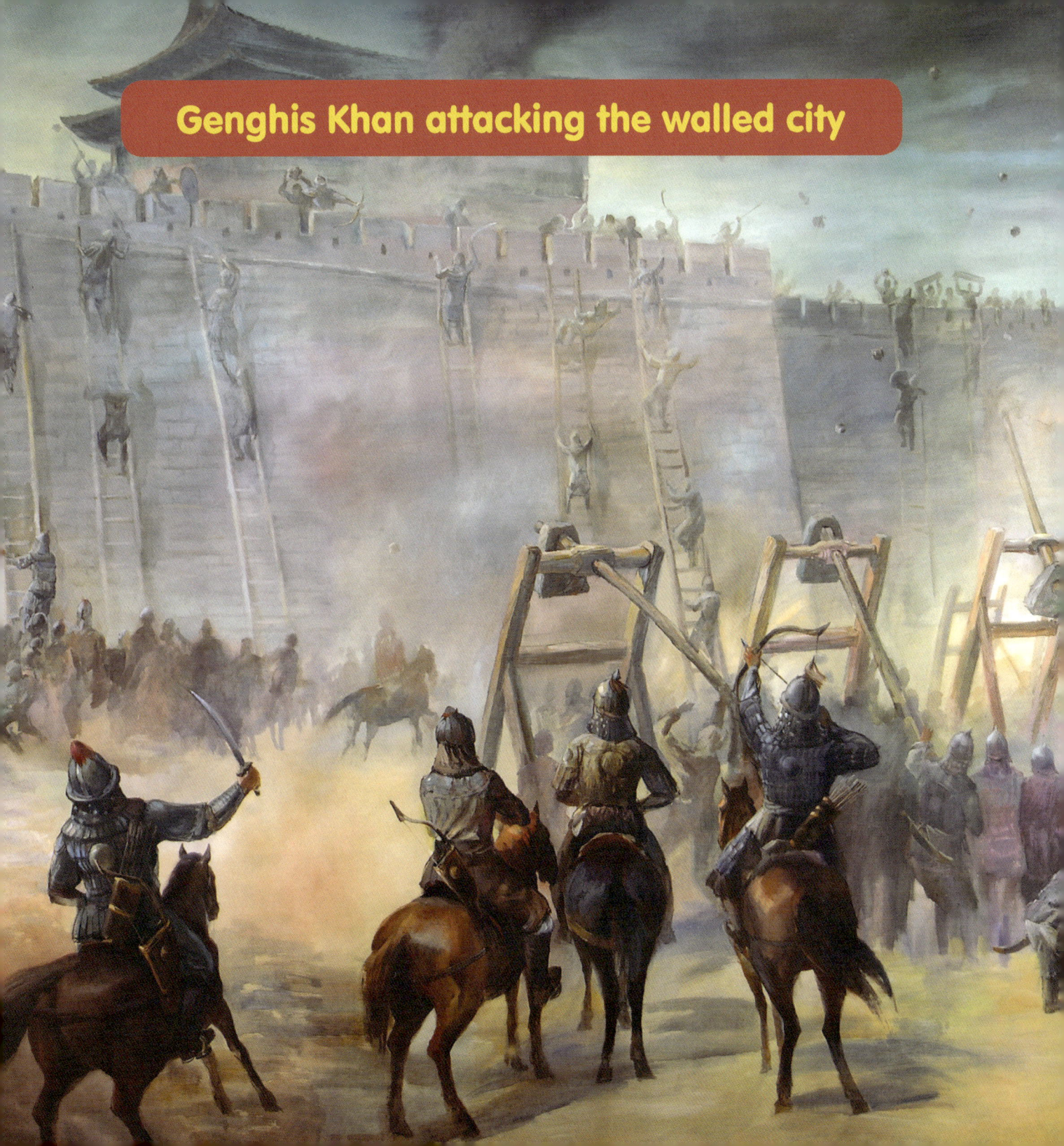

Genghis Khan attacking the walled city

Genghis Khan monument

CONQUESTS

Once the Mongol tribes were united, he turned to the south. In 1207, he attacked the Xi Xia people. It took him only two years to defeat the Xi Xia and they surrendered. He turned to China's Jin Dynasty in 1211. He wanted revenge for the way they treated the Mongols. He captured Yanjing (Beijing), Jin's capital city by 1215, and the Mongols now ruled the northern area of China.

Even though it is difficult to know definitively how many people died throughout the Mongol conquests, it is reported by historians that the number is approximately 40 million. The censuses obtained from the Middle Ages indicate that China's population plunged by tens of millions during his lifetime and some scholars believe that he killed three-fourths of Iran's modern day population during the time he was at war with the Khwarezmid Empire. All together, these attacks might have reduced the population of the world by 11 percent.

Statue of Genghis Khan at Marble Arch

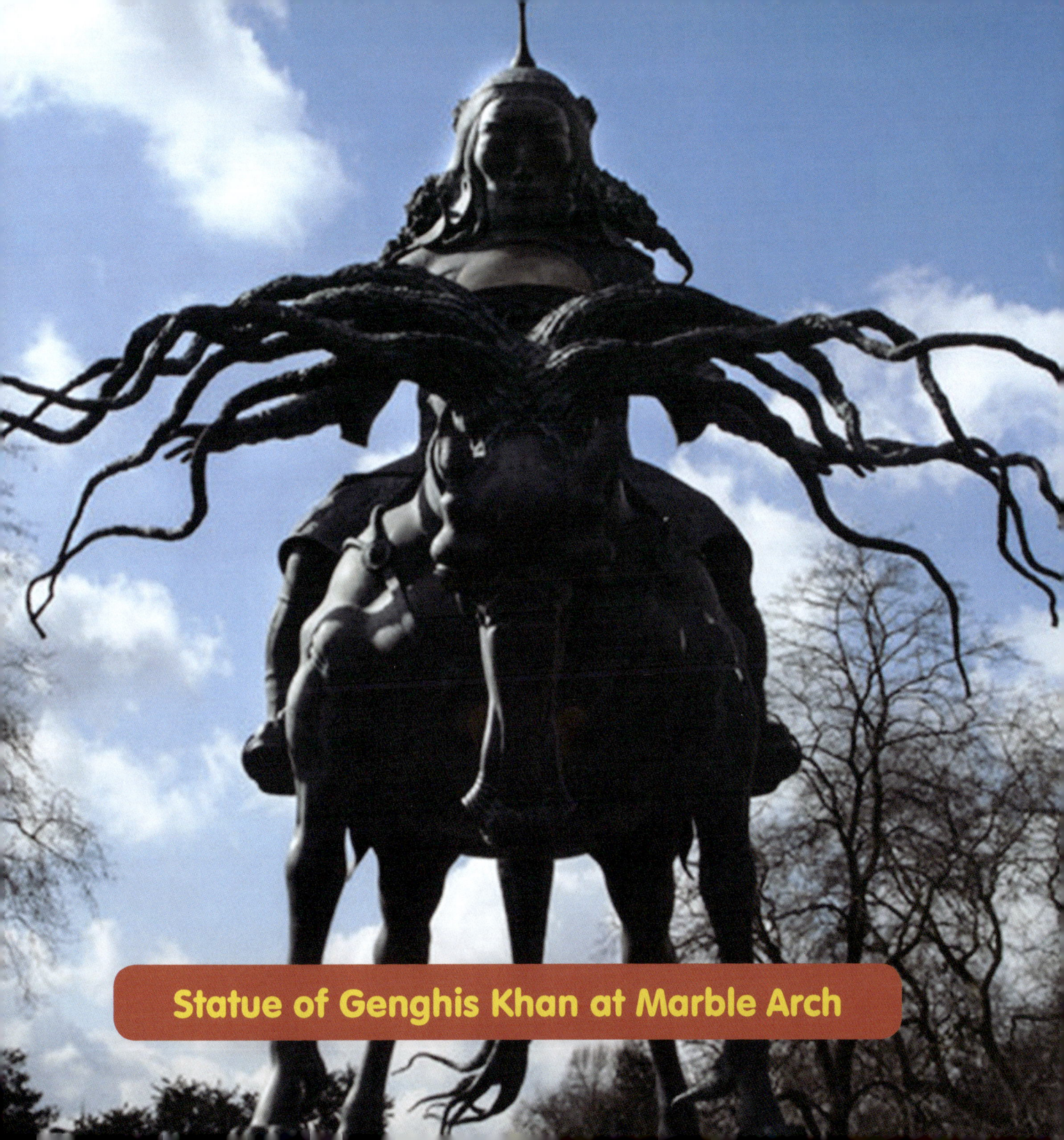

Genghis Khan mausoleum

MUSLIM LANDS

He desired establishment of trade with Muslim lands towards the west. A trade delegation was sent to for a meeting with its leaders. One city's governor, however, had the men killed. Genghis became furious.

He proceeded to take up command of 200,000 warriors and the next several years were spent destroying the western cities. He proceeded as far as Eastern Europe, destroying anything and everything. He became merciless, and left no one to live.

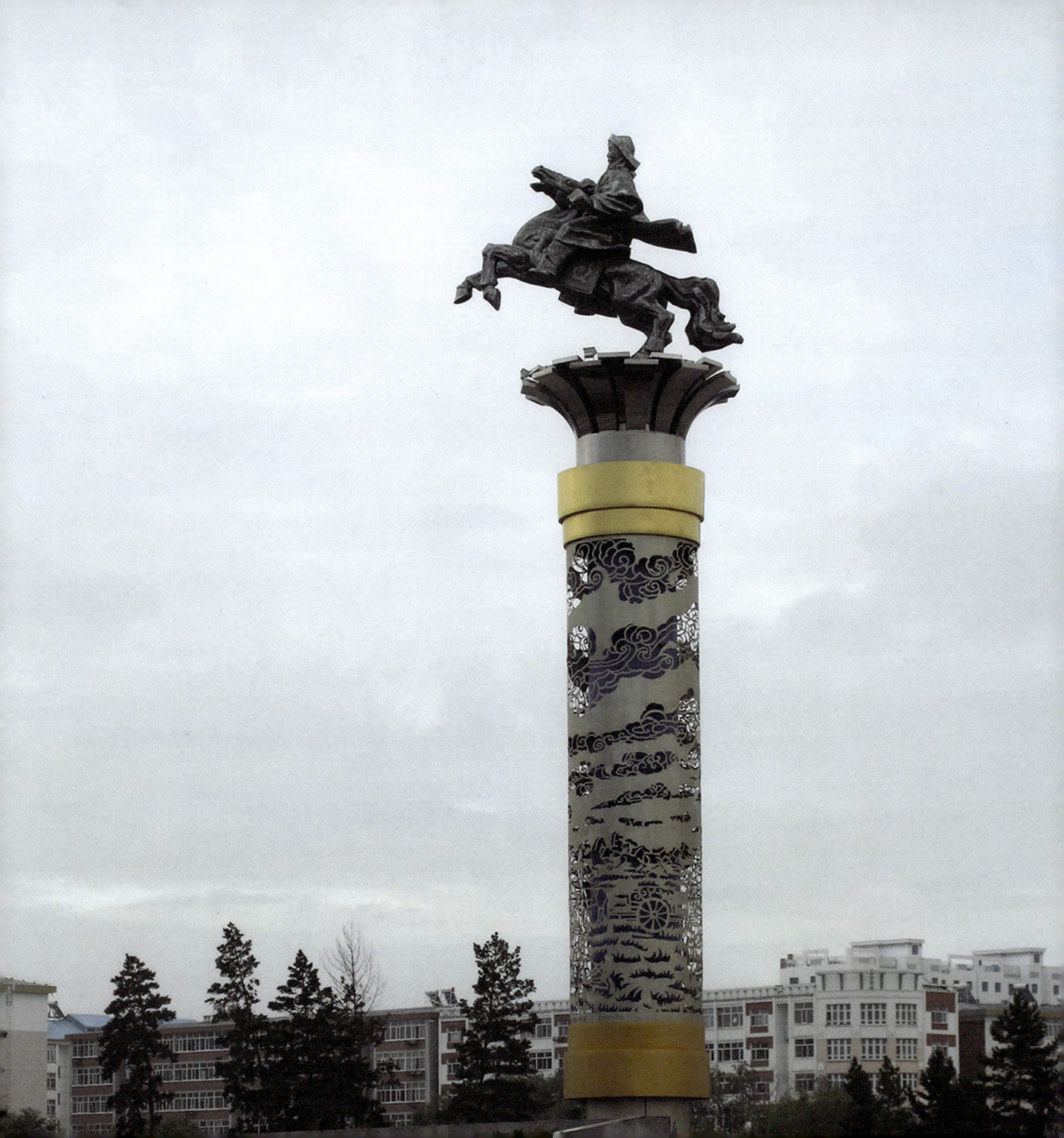

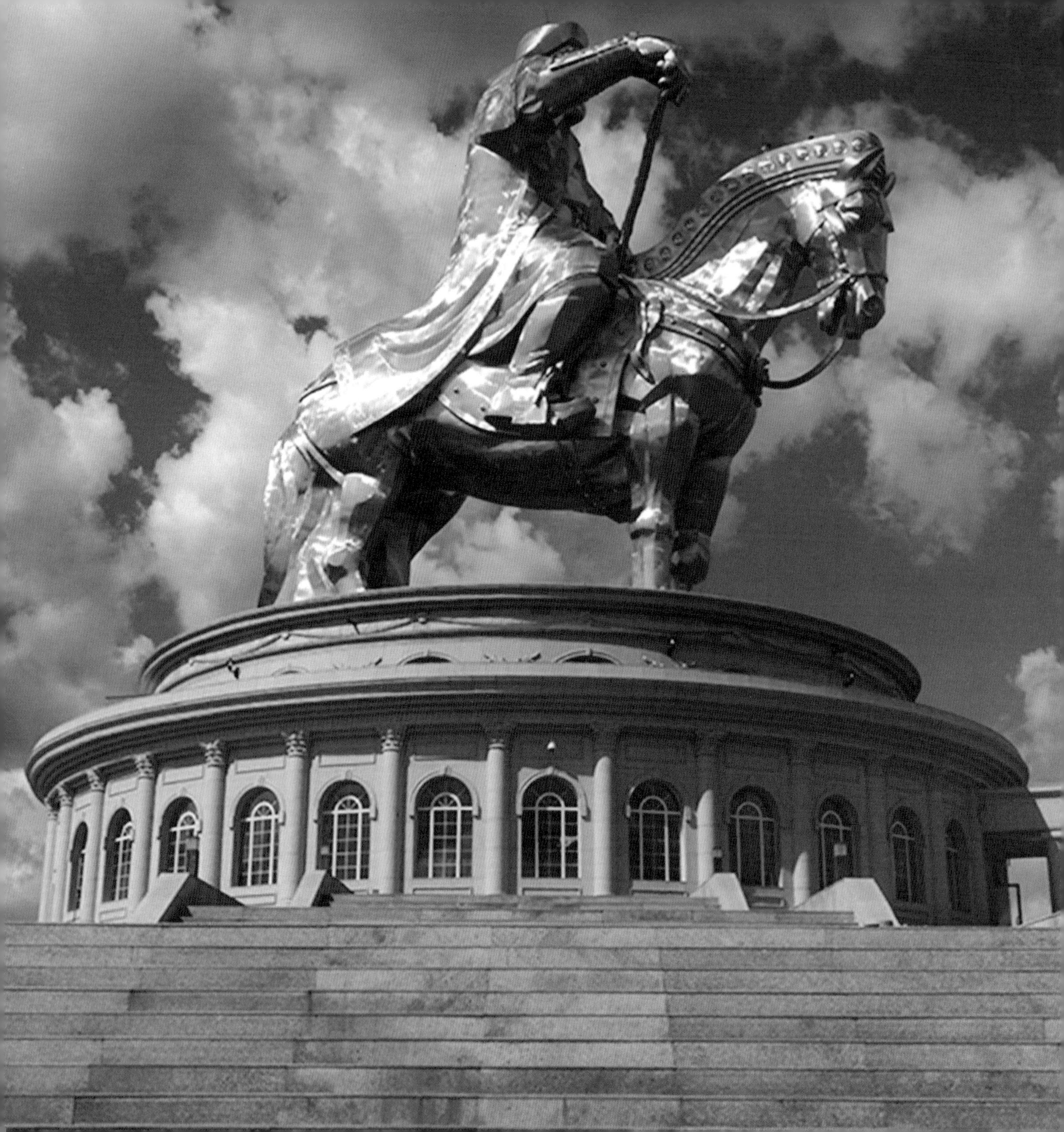

The Kwarizmian Empire was the name of the land towards the west. Its leader was Shah Ala ad-Din Muhammad. In 1221, this dynasty ended as he had both the Shah and his son killed.

DEATH

He died in 1227, after returning to China. Many believe that he injured himself as he fell from a horse, but no one knows for sure how he died. Other sources report anything from a wound to the knee by an arrow as well as malaria. Another more questionable account reports that he was murdered as he tried to rape a Chinese princess.

CHINGGIS KHAAN

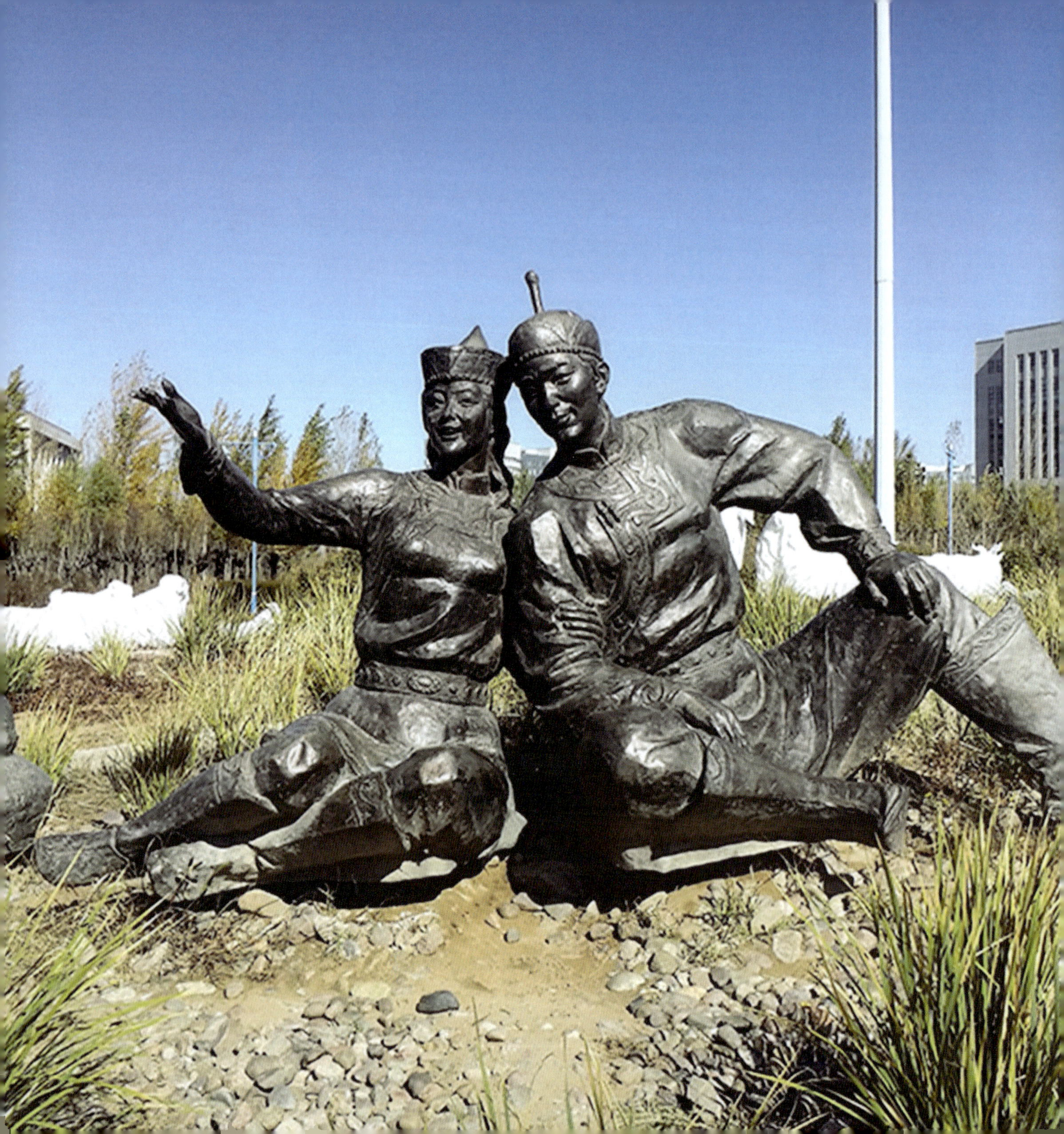

Once he died, however, we went to great lengths to keep secret his final place of rest. Legend indicates that during his funeral procession, everyone was slaughtered that they came into contact with so they would not be able to tell where he was to be buried.

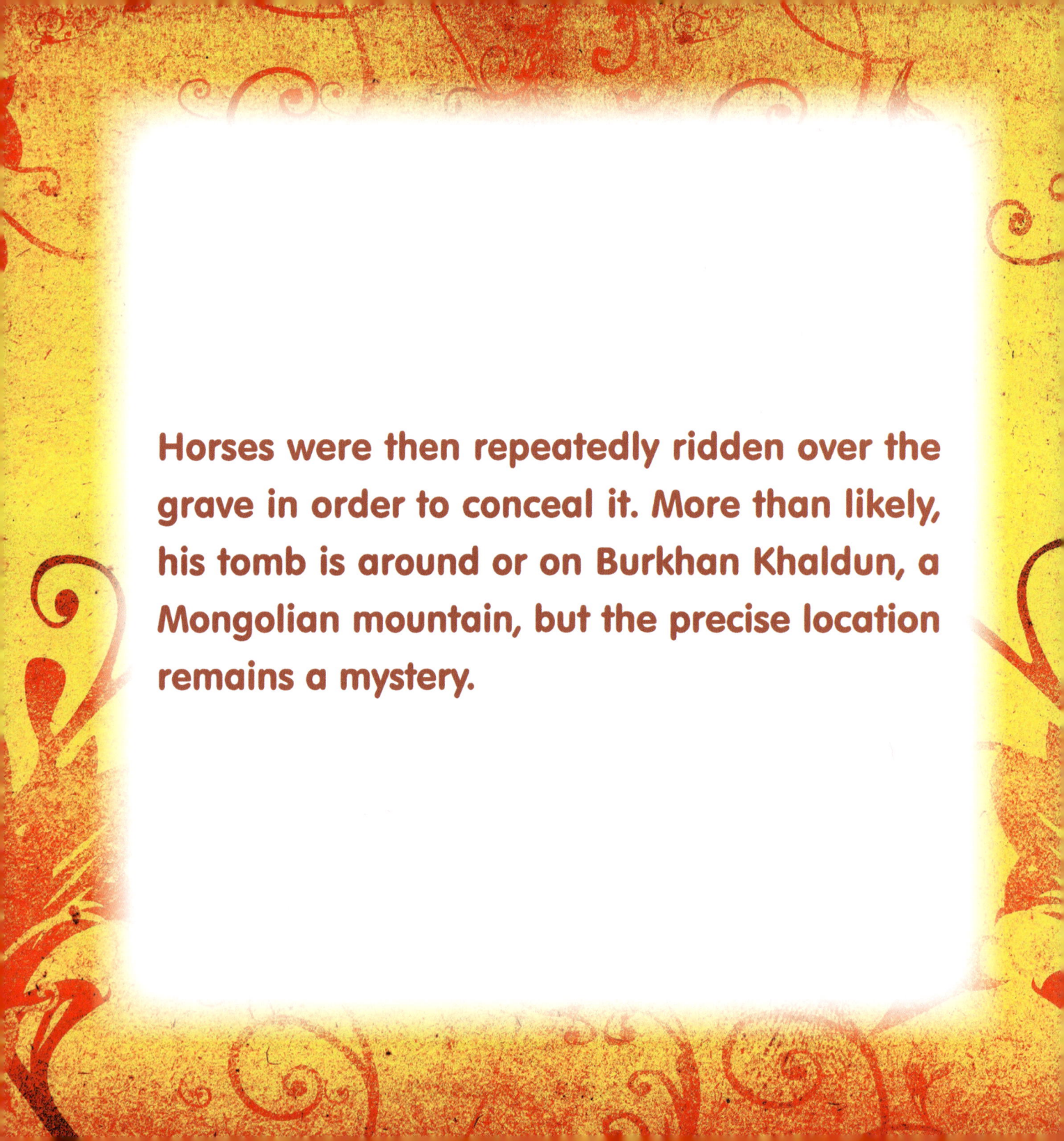

Horses were then repeatedly ridden over the grave in order to conceal it. More than likely, his tomb is around or on Burkhan Khaldun, a Mongolian mountain, but the precise location remains a mystery.

Burkhan Khaldun

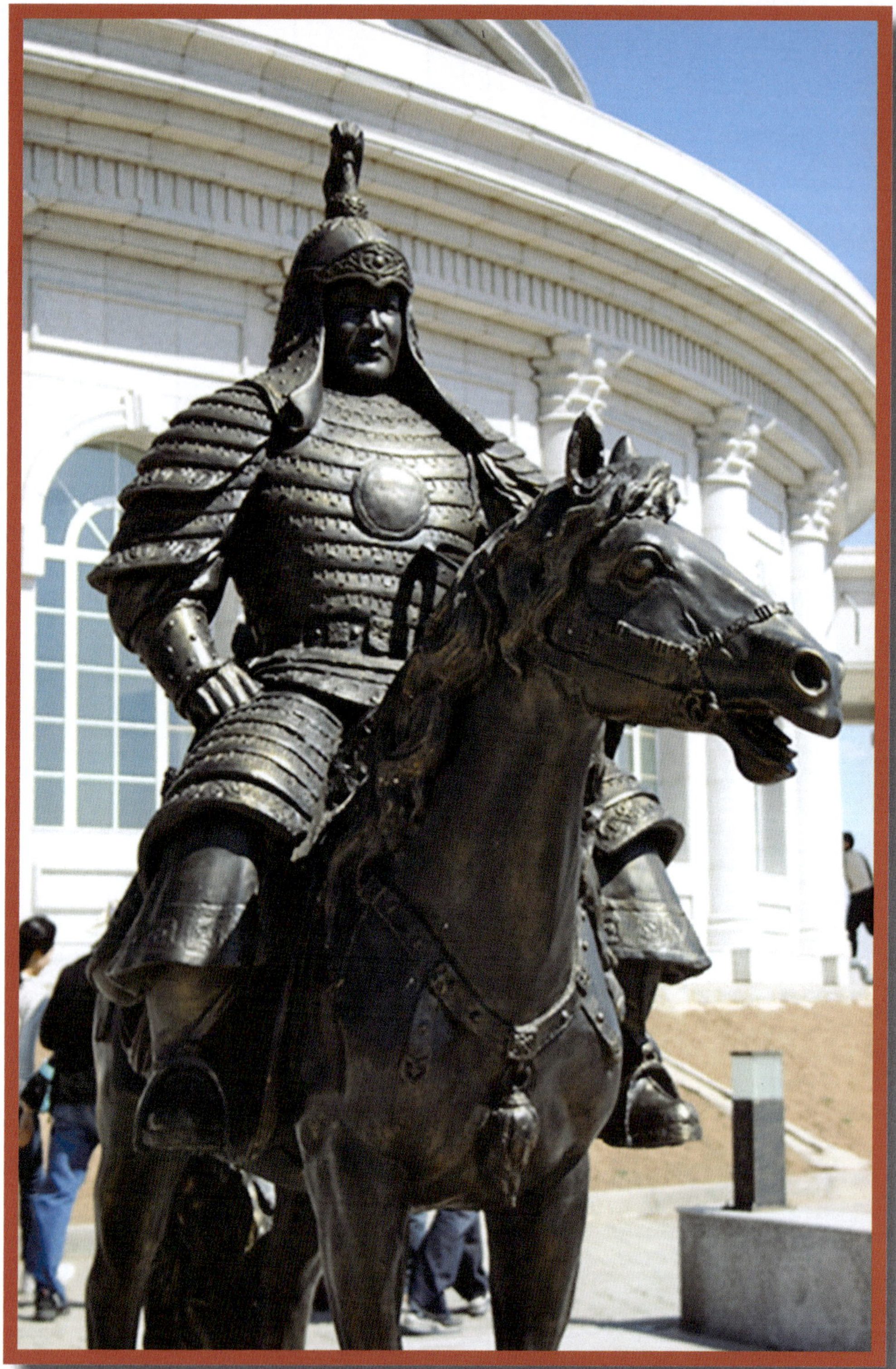

HIS LEGACY

Genghis Khan is now known to be a national hero and Mongolia's founding father. However, during the Soviet rule of the 20th century, merely mentioning his name had been banned.

Hopeful that they could erase all evidence of Mongolian nationalism, they tried suppressing his memory by forbidding people to make pilgrimage to Khentii, his birthplace, as well as deleting his story from textbooks.

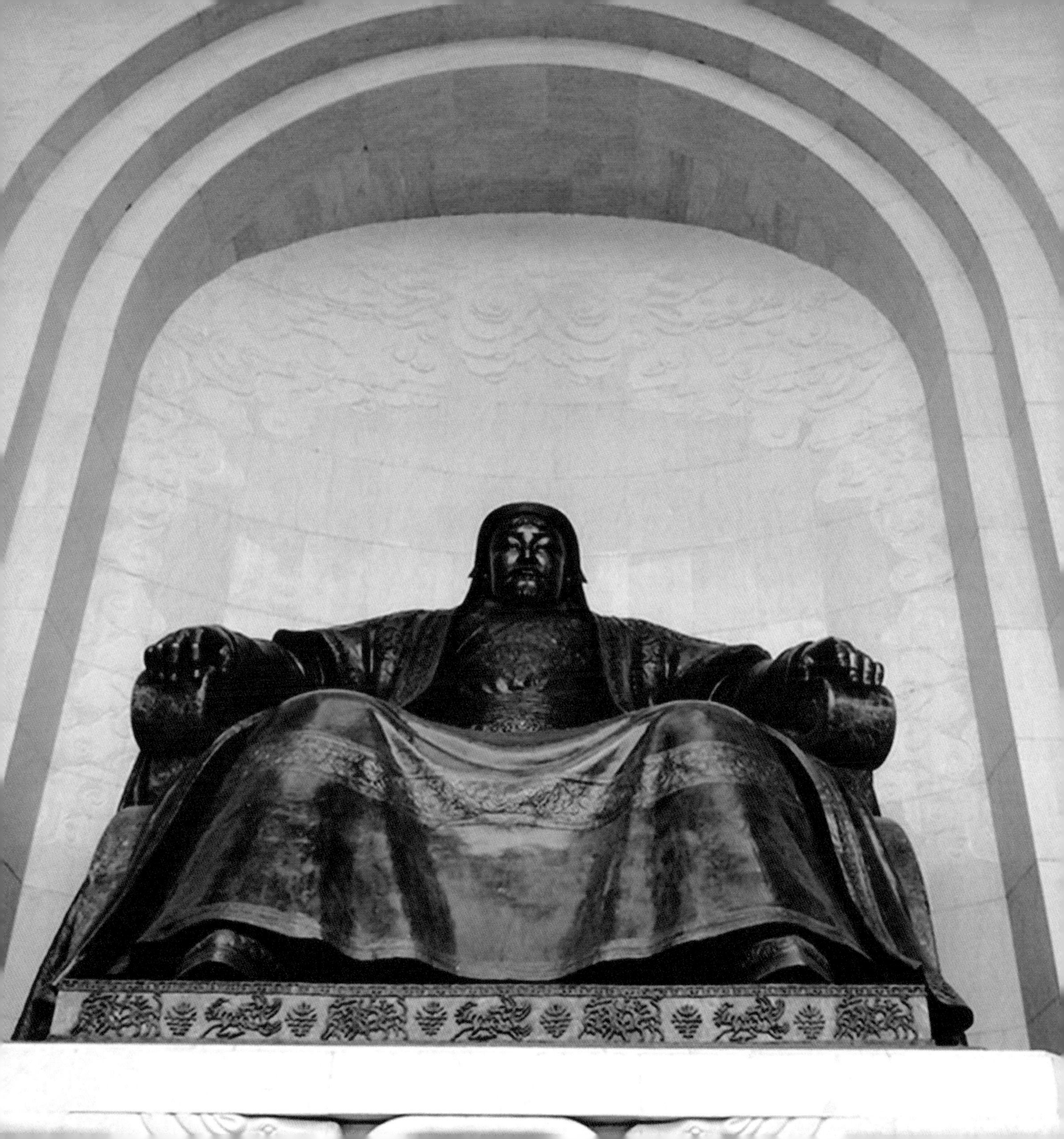

CHINGGIS KHAAN
INTERNATIONAL AIRPORT
ОЛОН УЛСЫН ИРЭХ НИСЛЭГ
INTERNATIONAL ARRIVALS
ОРОН НУТГИЙН ИРЭХ НИСЛ
DOMESTIC ARRIVALS

Eventually, his name was restored to Mongolian history after winning independence early in the 1990s. He has since become recurring in popular culture and art. His portrait now appears on its currency and the nation's airport in Ulan Bator is named for him.

His legacy is significant. His successors, including Kublai Khan who was his grandson, completed conquest of China and maintained control over it from many years. Ogedei, Genghis' immediate successor, ruled the Mongol Empire during its greatest extent, from Korea in the east to Poland in the west, approximately 11 million square miles, comparable to the size of Africa. One benefit of this seizure was consolidation of rule over Silk Road, streamlining communication and trade between West and East.

Kublai Khan

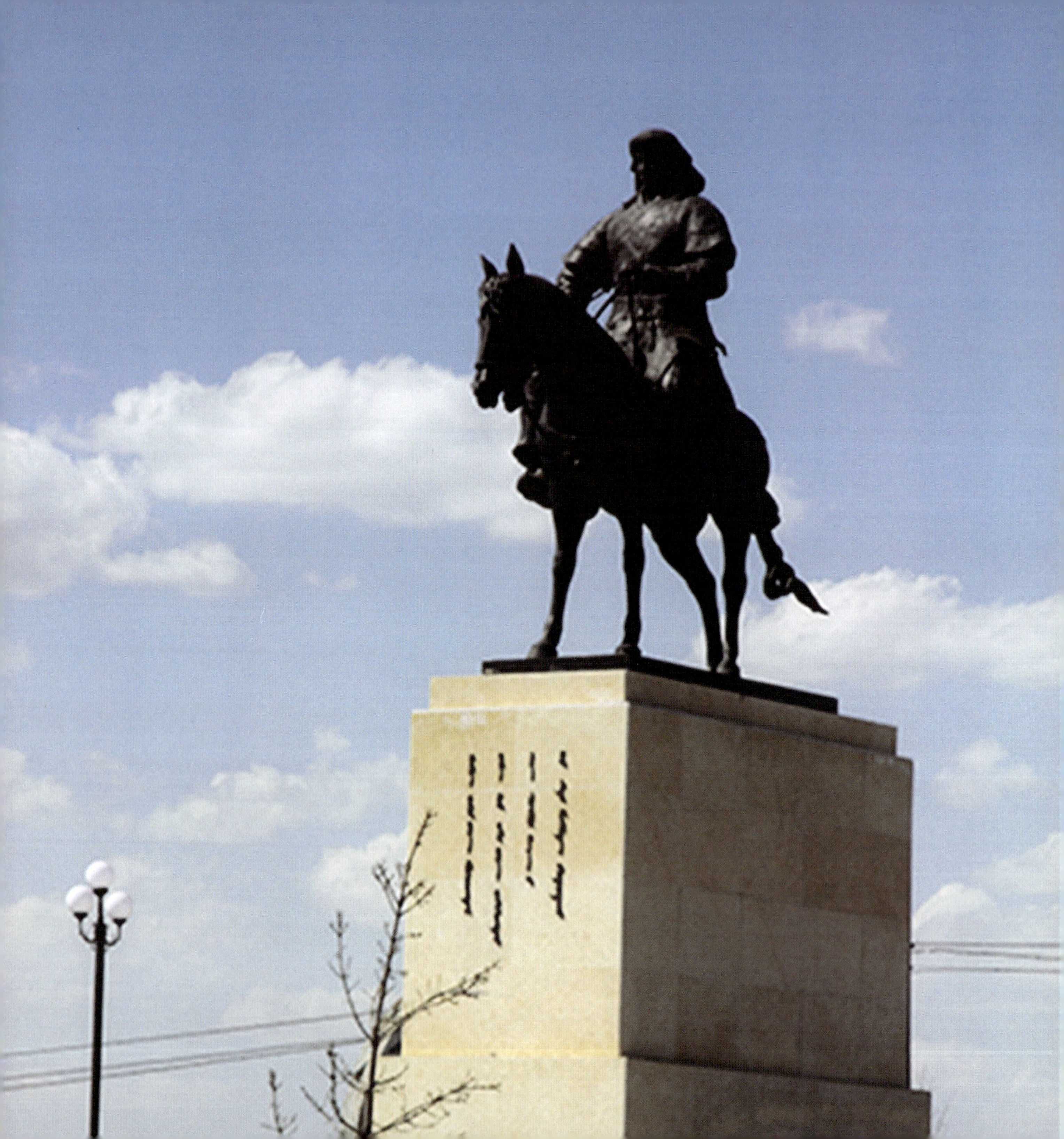

Genghis was known to be an intolerant and brutal man, creating death and destruction. The people he conquered felt negatively towards him because of his brutality.

As you have learned, Genghis Khan was a very powerful leader, but was he mean? Think about it and decide for yourself. For additional information go to your local library, research the internet, and ask questions of your teachers, family, and friends.

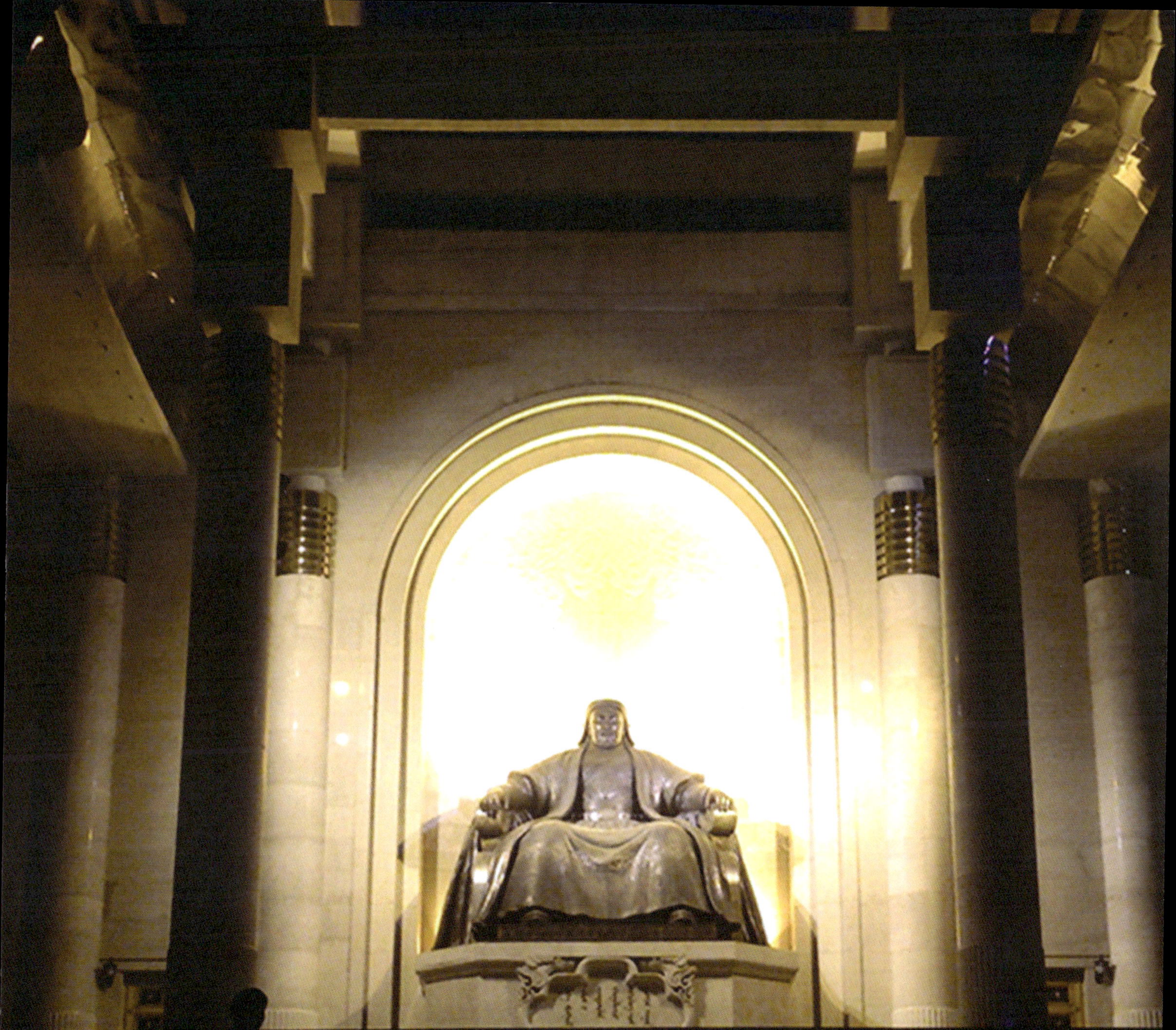

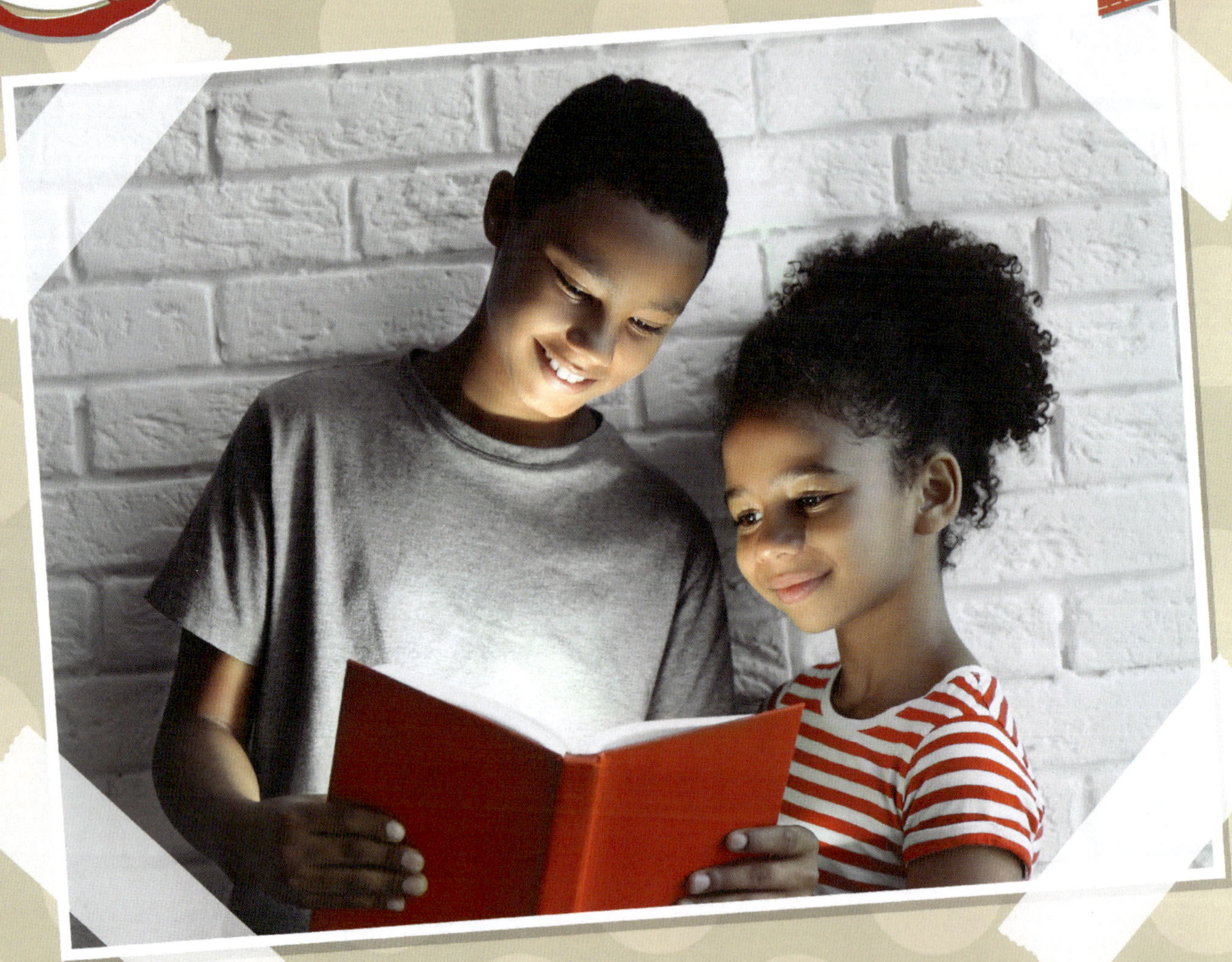

Visit

BABY PROFESSOR
EDUCATION KIDS

www.BabyProfessorBooks.com

to download Free Baby Professor eBooks and view our catalog of new and exciting Children's Books

Printed in Great Britain
by Amazon

YOGA DIET RECIPES

+50 Simple & Nourishing Vegan Recipes

Gabrielle Baker

All rights reserved.
Disclaimer

The information contained i is meant to serve as a comprehensive collection of strategies that the author of this eBook has done research about. Summaries, strategies, tips and tricks are only recommendation by the author, and reading this eBook will not guarantee that one's results will exactly mirror the author's results. The author of the eBook has made all reasonable effort to provide current and accurate information for the readers of the eBook. The author and it's associates will not be held liable for any unintentional error or omissions that may be found. The material in the eBook may include information by third parties. Third party materials comprise of opinions expressed by their owners. As such, the author of the eBook does not assume responsibility or liability for any third party material or opinions. Whether because of the progression of the internet, or the unforeseen changes in company policy and editorial submission guidelines, what is stated as fact at the time of this writing may become outdated or inapplicable later.

The eBook is copyright © 2021 with all rights reserved. It is illegal to redistribute, copy, or create derivative work from this eBook whole or in part. No parts of this report may be reproduced or retransmitted in any reproduced or retransmitted in any forms whatsoever without the writing expressed and signed permission from the author.

INTRODUCTION 6
BREAKFAST 12
   Yogi Tea 13
   Artichoke Water 16
   Golden Almond & Turmeric Milk 18
   Hangover Helper Scramble 21
   Semolina & Carom Pancakes 23
   Goji & Chia Strawberry smoothie bowl 27
   Millet waffles with chocolate syrup and flax seeds 29
   Breakfast of Cheerful Champs 33
   Tofu & Kales scramble 34
   Tortilla 38
   Fruit and Quinoa Protein Oats 39
   Yogic Carrot Juice 42
   Blueberry & Greek Yogurt Muffins 43
   Fruit and Coconut Milk Smoothie 47
   Slumbery Smoothie 50
   Success Smoothie 51
   Cucumber Chili Coolers 52
MAIN DISH 56
   Mung Beans & Rice with Vegetables 57
   Black Eye Bean & Coconut Curry 59

Golden Fish	68
Salmon Crush Crunch	69
Quinoa Tabouli	71
Puffed Millet, Rice & Pomegranate	73
Spanish chickpeas and pasta	76
Tamarind Fish Curry	80
Chili Scallops in Coconut Milk	84
Okra Curry	87
Vegetable Coconut Curry	89
Malabari Chili Fish with Chili Chutney	92
Semolina with Vegetables	95
Cheesy Beet-Carrot Casserole	98
Pumpkin Curry with spicy seeds	101
Creamy Almond Chicken	104
Hot Spiced Lamb	108
Lobster Thermidor in Nutty Sauce	111
Red Chili Fish Fry	115
Salmon in Saffron-Flavored Curry	118
Pork Bafat	121
Fish in a Velvety Serrano Sauce	124
Spicy Shrimp in Coconut Milk	127
Parsi Fish	131
Wasabi Chicken Tikka	134

Chicken with Nuts in a Creamy Sauce 136
VEGAN CURRIES 140
- Basic Vegetable Curry 141
- Cabbage Curry 144
- Cauliflower Curry 148
- Cauliflower and Potato Curry 150
- Okra / Ladies Finger Curry 156
- Potato Curry – Boiled 158
- Potato Curry – Raw 160
- Potato, Cauliflower & Tomato Curry 162
- Pumpkin Curry 164
- Stir Fry Vegetables 165
- Tomato Curry 166
- White Gourd Curry 169

INTRODUCTION

There is an instinct within all of us to follow a clean and healthy eating lifestyle. Deep down inside we know what is good and what is not good for us but at times chose to ignore the body and mind. Regular practice of yoga helps to stimulate these natural instincts. Yoga changes the habits and is a process of normalization.

The main purpose of food should be to give energy to the body and mind, increase the resistance power of the body and to develop the mind. Fresh food gives lightness, happiness, joyfulness and increases intelligence. Food should be suitable for the mind, body, intelligence and soul.

There are no special dietary rules for asana practitioners although there are many recommendations with the main ones being to eat natural foods and eat in moderation. Yoga advises a vegetarian diet, particularly as it is preparation for the higher forms of yoga. Vegetarianism has been found to promote inner calmness and harmony between the body and mind, whilst eating meat has been linked with inner tension, anger, disharmony and an increase in desires. Vegetarianism is the basis of a sattwic diet.

A yogic diet ideally follows a sattwic or pure food

diet. A balance of fresh fruit, vegetables, cooked whole grains, milk, legumes, nuts and seeds, using a combination of both raw and cooked foods. These foods increase sattwa in the body because they are light, simple and supply all the necessary nutrients. They increase our physical and mental vitality making it easier to experience clarity, lightness and peace of mind. Rajasic foods are prepared with much oil and spice. They create heaviness and restlessness in the mind. Meat and fish are classified under these. Onion and garlic are also under this group as they increase desire. Tamasic foods are foods that are old and stale. They lower the energy and cause laziness. They include foods that are not cooked properly or chewed well and processed foods.

Stale, processed and frozen foods have lost their pranic energy. If we try to eat only sattwic foods as much as possible we can slowly change the body chemistry, renewing the digestive system and taking away any strain. Ideally we should eat foods that take minimum energy to digest, so that the remaining energy can be used for more productive uses.

When eating it is important to fill the stomach half full with food. A quarter should be left for water or liquids. The last quarter should be left empty for digestion to take place. This space is necessary for the stomach to churn the food with the digestive juices. It is also said in Hindu culture that this last quarter should be left for Lord Shiva.

Eat to satisfy hunger without getting any feelings of heaviness or laziness. It is said that you should eat only what is needed. To find out how much you need to eat do an experiment. One time eat until you have a feeling of fullness, being aware of how much you are eating. From there half the amount of food, this is your requirement. There should be enough space in the stomach so that if somebody asked you to eat a meal with them after you had already finished your meal you could do it without any ill effects.

The timing of meals should be fixed. In this way the body begins to release digestive secretions at a certain time. It is important not to skip meals so that the body doesn't keep going into panic mode and decide to store excess fat. Change the diet according to the seasons. Don't eat imported foods. Always try to eat what is local and fresh. If you know your dosha/prakriti then makes your food choices accordingly. Don't eat when negative, angry or depressed. How you are thinking effects your digestion. You should only eat when you are happy and peaceful. When you eat focus, feel and appreciate every mouthful, eating slowly and being thankful for the food that has been given to you. Remember, eat to live, and don't live to eat.

We must start with the basics, the essentials for our survival, if we wish to achieve anything in yoga. Diet and food are among these. We can only really begin to live the full yogic lifestyle when we have gone through the first layers of our needs, desires, intuitions and instincts, preparing us for the physical, mental, psychic and spiritual levels.

Best Yogic Ingredients for Clean Eating

These three potent roots, known as the Trinity Roots, are essential for cleansing, sustaining, and producing energy in the body.

Garlic
- Fights viruses and bacteria.
- Increases sexual energy that, with the practice of Kundalini Yoga, can be channeled upward for greater spiritual awareness.
- Eat raw, baked, steamed, or in capsule form.

Onion
- Universal healing food.
- Purifies and builds new blood.
- Recommended for colds, fever, laryngitis, and diarrhea.
- Increases mental clarity.
- Eat raw (preferred), juiced, or cooked.

Ginger Root
- Soothes and strengthens nerves by nourishing spinal fluid.
- Increases energy and vitality.
- Useful for menstruating women.
- Drink as a tea or juice or use it as a spice in main dishes.

Turmeric

- Good for the skin and mucous membranes.
- Good for female reproductive organs.
- Increases bone and joint flexibility, anti-inflammatory.
- Sauté for curries, casseroles, soups, gravies, and sauces.

Yogi Tea
- Black pepper purifies the blood.
- Cinnamon strengthens the bones.
- Cardamom supports the colon.
- Cloves build the nervous system.
- Ginger, with all its benefits, is an optional addition.
- Black tea (tiny amount) holds it all together.
- Milk protects the colon.

BREAKFAST

Yogi Tea

Yogi Tea is health promoting, delicious and soothing and a great coffee substitute. Yogi Tea helps in the easy assimilation of spices by acting as an alloy for all the ingredients, creating just the right chemical balance.

Ingredients:
For each cup:
- 10 ounces of water (about 1 1/3 cups)
- 3 whole cloves
- 4 whole green cardamom pods, cracked
- 4 whole black peppercorns
- $\frac{1}{2}$ stick cinnamon
- $\frac{1}{4}$ teaspoon black tea
- $\frac{1}{2}$ cup milk
- 2 slices fresh ginger root

Directions:
Bring water to a boil and add spices. Cover and boil 15 to 20 minutes, then add black tea. Let sit for a few minutes, then add the milk and return to a boil. Don't let it boil over.

When it reaches a boil, remove immediately from heat, strain, and sweeten with honey, if desired.

Nutrition
Calories: 0

Carbs: 0g
Fat: 0g
Protein: 0g

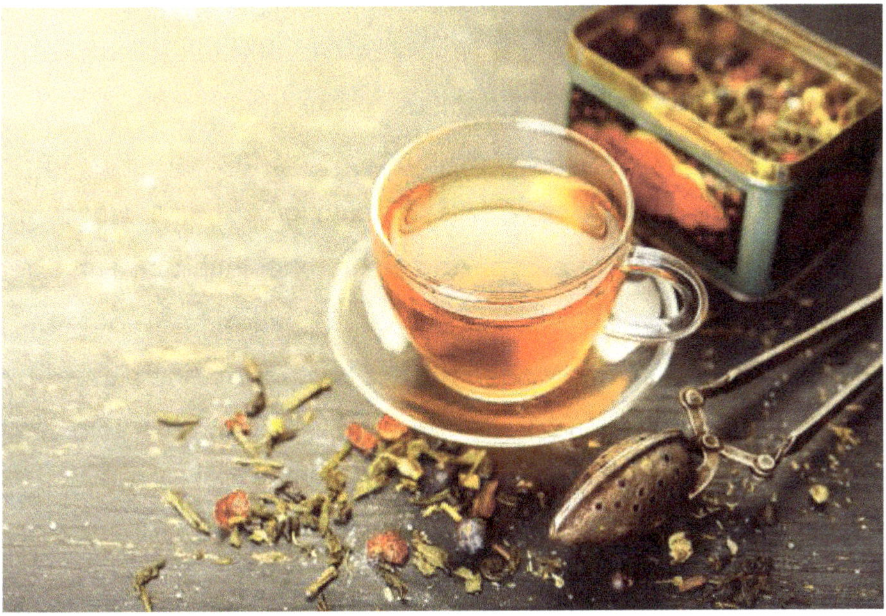

Artichoke Water

- 2 artichokes

Cut the stems off the artichokes and cut the top inch off of the leaves. Fill a large pot with water and bring to a boil. Add artichokes and boil for 30 minutes, or until you can easily pull off the bottom leaves of the artichoke. Remove artichokes and save for a snack. Let the water cool and then drink a cup of it. This will help your liver detoxify itself and your entire body.

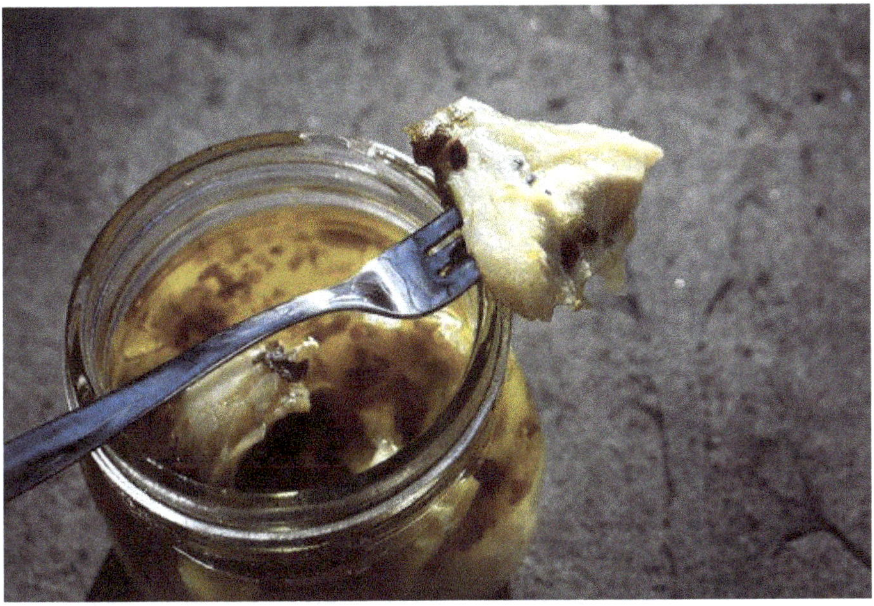

Golden Almond & Turmeric Milk

This beverage is especially beneficial for stiff joints and provides a source of lubrication for the entire system.

Ingredients:
- 1/8 teaspoon turmeric
- ¼ cup water 8 ounces milk
- 2 tablespoons raw almond oil
- Honey to taste

Directions:
Simmer turmeric in water until it forms a nice paste. Suggested cooking time is 8 minutes, you can add more water as necessary. Meanwhile, bring milk to a boil with the almond oil. As soon as it boils, remove from heat. Combine the two mixtures.

Add honey to taste.

Nutrition
Serving size: 1 cup
Calories: 45
Fat: 2.5 g
Carbohydrates: 5 g
Sugar: 2.5 g
Fiber: 1.5 g
Protein: 1 g

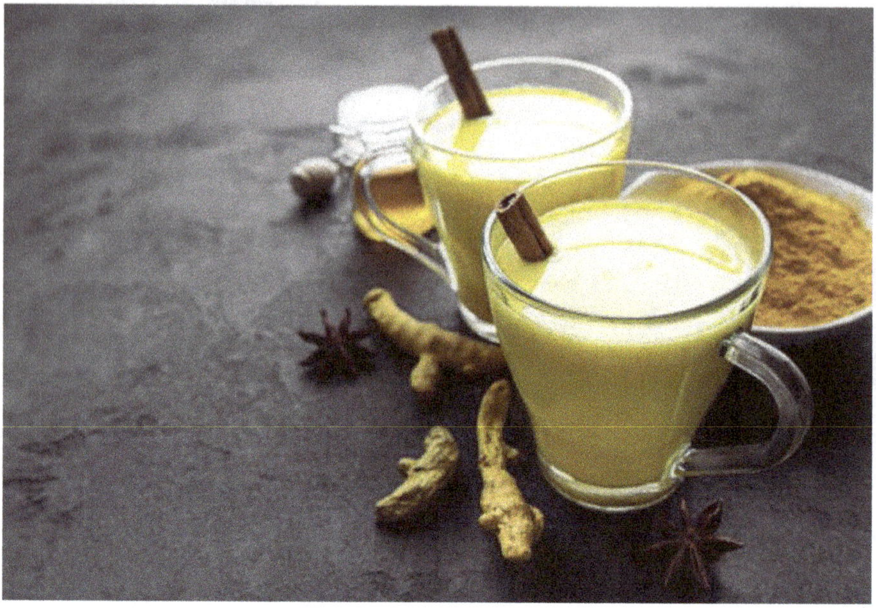

Hangover Helper Scramble

- 3 eggs
- 1 teaspoon olive oil
- 4 asparagus spears
- ½ cup cherry or grape tomatoes, cut in half or quarters
- Black pepper, to taste

Crack the three eggs in a bowl and scramble. Heat the oil in a small frying pan. Add asparagus and tomatoes and cook until asparagus are soft. Add egg and cook until set. Top with freshly ground black pepper, if desired.

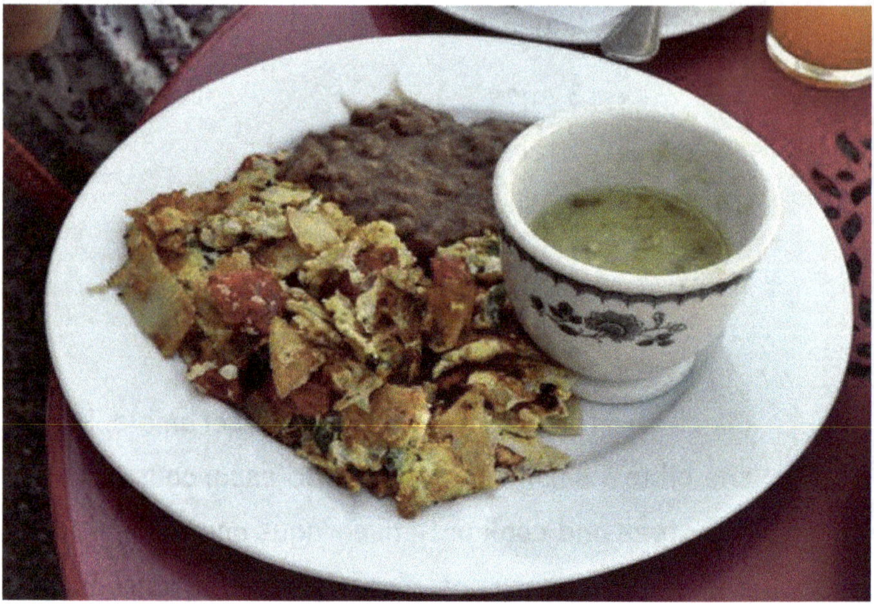

Semolina & Carom Pancakes

This mild recipe is perfect for a Sunday morning breakfast. Serve these with tangy Tamarind Chutney

Serves 4
Prep Time: 20 minutes
Cook Time: 15 minutes

Ingredients
- 1 cup coarse semolina or plain cream of wheat
- 1 cup plain yogurt
- Salt, to taste
- Water at room temperature, as needed
- 1/4 teaspoon baking powder
- 1/4 teaspoon carom seeds
- 1/4 small red onion, peeled and finely chopped
- small red bell pepper, seeded and finely chopped
- 1/2 small tomato, seeded and finely chopped
- tablespoons vegetable oil

Directions
Combine the semolina, yogurt, and salt in a medium-sized mixing bowl; mix well. Add 1/4 to 1/2 cup water to reach the consistency of pancake batter, ensuring that you do not have any lumps in the

batter. Add the baking powder. Set aside for about 20 minutes.

In a separate bowl, create the topping. Mix the carom seeds, onions, bell peppers, and tomatoes. Heat a griddle on medium-low. Add a few drops of oil. Ladle about 1/4 cup of batter into the center of the griddle. It should have the thickness of a regular pancake. As the batter starts to cook, bubbles will begin to appear on the surface.

Add a small amount of topping to the pancake, while it is still moist. Press down gently with the back of your ladle. Add a few drops of oil around the sides of the pancakes to keep it from sticking.

Flip the pancake over and cook the other side for about 2 minutes. Remove the pancake from heat and place on a serving platter. Continue this until all the batter is used up. Serve warm.

Nutrition
165 Calories
27g Carbs
0 Fats
7g Protein

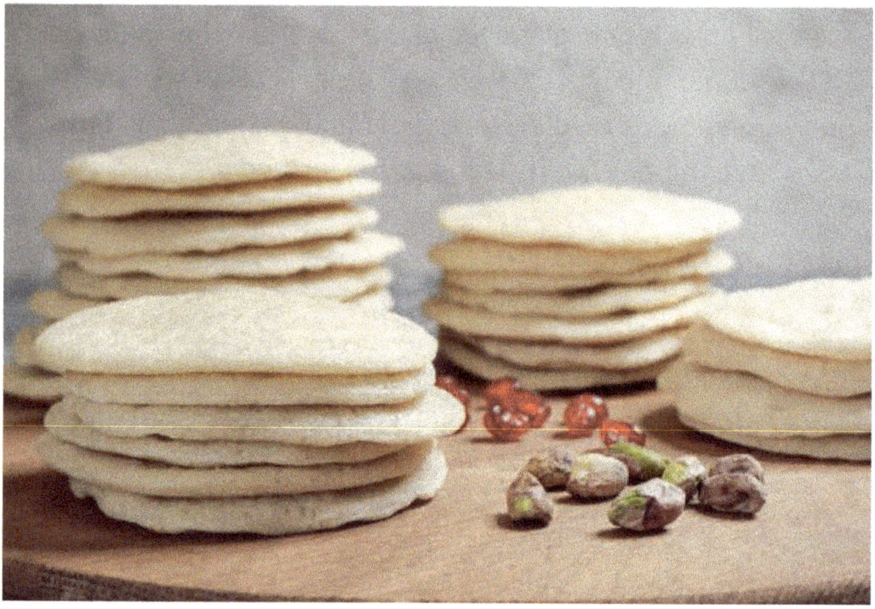

Goji & Chia Strawberry smoothie bowl

Total Time: 5 minutes
Yield: 1

Ingredients

- 1T goji berries
- 1T Strawberries
- 1-inch piece cinnamon stick
- 2-4T chia seeds
- 1 T coconut oil
- 16 oz. coconut water
- 2T cashew milk yogurt
- 1/3 c hemp seeds
- 2-3 large kale leaves
- 1c frozen berries
- ½ frozen banana

Directions

Place goji berries, cinnamon, and chia seeds in your blender, and add enough coconut water to cover well. Let soak about 10 minutes. Add the remaining coconut water and the rest of the ingredients to the blender and process on the appropriate setting for smoothies, adding extra liquid (coconut water, water, or nut milk) for your desired consistency.

Nutrition
Calories 150,
Total Fat 8g
Total Carbs 14g
Fiber 4g
Protein 6g

Millet waffles with chocolate syrup and flax seeds

Waffles are better than pancakes because they've got all those nooks and crannies waiting to be filled with goodness! They're also great for special occasions and lazy Sunday mornings, but if you freeze them you can pop them in the toaster for those less-lazy days of the week. Drizzle with syrup and sprinkle flax seeds. You will need to soak the grains overnight, so make sure you plan accordingly.

Yield: 4

Ingredients

- 1c millet
- 1c untoasted buckwheat, or whole oats
- ¼ c flax seeds
- ¼ c shredded unsweetened coconut flakes (optional)
- 2 T blackstrap molasses or agave
- 2 T unrefined coconut oil
- ½ t salt
- 1-3 t ground cinnamon
- 1-3 t orange zest (optional)

- ¼ c sunflower seeds (optional)
- Chocolate syrup

Directions

Place millet, buckwheat (or oats), and flax in a small bowl, add water to cover by an inch, and let stand overnight.

Strain and discard the soaking water. (It'll be gooey!) Place the grains in a blender, preferably not a high-speed one, but if, like me, that's all you've got, no worries—the waffles may just come out denser.

Add water to barely cover the grains (about 1½ cups). Then add the rest of the ingredients except the sunflower seeds. Blend into a thick batter. Some millet will remain whole and provide a nice crunch.

Pour some batter into a hot waffle iron. Sprinkle the batter with sunflower seeds (if using), close, and bake according to the manufacturer's directions.

Serve with or without your favorite toppings.

You can refrigerate batter for up to five days.

Nutrition

Calories 181
Total Fat 6.8 g
Total Carbohydrates 26.3 g
Dietary Fiber 3.9 g
Protein 5.3 g

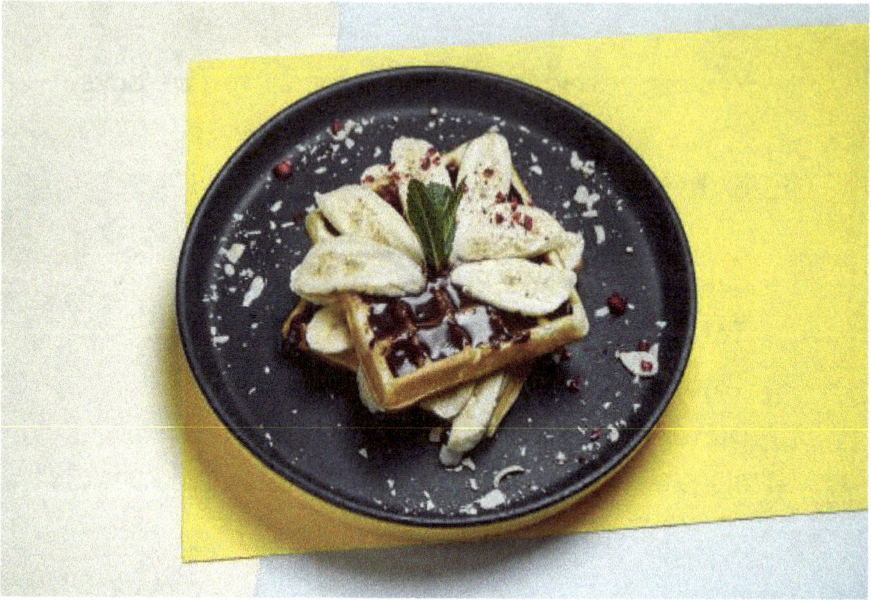

Breakfast of Cheerful Champs

Eat a wedge of this frittata for breakfast every morning.

- 8 organic eggs
- 1 tablespoon extra virgin olive oil
- 1 cup baby spinach
- 1 cup shiitake mushrooms, diced
- 1 cup chopped broccoli
- Salt and pepper, to taste

Crack eggs into a large bowl and whisk. Set aside. Heat oil in a large oven-proof pan over medium heat. Add spinach, mushrooms, broccoli, and salt and pepper, and cook until the vegetables are soft. Pour eggs into pan and cook, undisturbed, until the sides set, about 2 minutes. Cover and cook 10 to 13 minutes until set. Slide onto a plate and cut into wedges.

Tofu & Kales scramble

Savory, Southwest-inspired tofu scrambles for 1 with lots of veggies and a simple 5-ingredient sauce

PREP TIME 10 minutes
COOK TIME 20 minutes
TOTAL TIME 30 minutes
Servings 2

Ingredients

- 8 ounces extra-firm tofu
- 1-2 Tbsp olive oil
- 1/4 red onion (thinly sliced)
- 1/2 red pepper (thinly sliced)
- 2 cups kale (loosely chopped)

Sauce
- 1/2 tbsp sea salt (reduce amount for less salty sauce)
- 1/2 tbsp garlic powder
- 1/2 tbsp ground cumin
- 1/4 tbsp chili powder
- Water (to thin)
- 1/4 tbsp turmeric (optional)

For serving (optional)
- Salsa
- Cilantro
- Hot Sauce

- Breakfast potatoes, toast, and/or fruit

Directions

Pat tofu dry and roll in a clean, absorbent towel with something heavy on top, such as a cast-iron skillet, for 15 minutes.

While tofu is draining, prepare sauce by adding dry spices to a small bowl and adding enough water to make a pourable sauce. Set aside.

Prep veggies and warm a large skillet over medium heat. Once hot, add olive oil and the onion and red pepper. Season with a pinch each salt and pepper and stir. Cook until softened – about 5 minutes.

Add kale, season with a bit more salt and pepper, and cover to steam for 2 minutes.

In the meantime, unwrap tofu and use a fork to crumble into bite-sized pieces.

Use a spatula to move the veggies to one side of the pan and add tofu. Sauté for 2 minutes, then add sauce, pouring it mostly over the tofu and a little over the veggies. Stir immediately, evenly distributing the sauce. Cook for another 5-7 minutes until tofu is slightly browned.

Serve immediately with the breakfast potatoes, toast, or fruit. I like to add more flavor with salsa, hot sauce, and/or fresh cilantro. Alternatively, freeze for up to 1 month and reheat on the stovetop or in the microwave.

Video

Nutrition (1 of 2 servings)
Serving: 1 serving
Calories: 212
Carbohydrates: 7.1 g
Protein: 16.4 g
Fat: 15.1 g
Fiber: 2.1 g

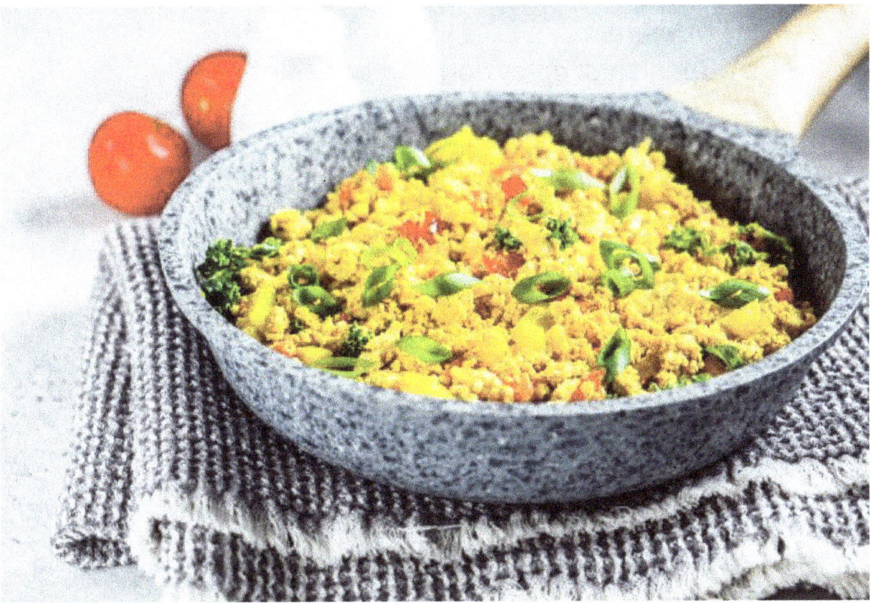

Tortilla

A Spanish staple, done an easy Retox way.

- 2 teaspoons extra virgin olive oil
- 1 yellow onion, chopped
- 2 zucchinis, chopped
- 8 eggs (or 6 egg whites and 3 whole eggs)
- Dash of salt

Heat oil in a large pan over medium heat. Add onion and let cook until soft. Add zucchini and stir, lower heat, and cover. While the vegetables are cooking, beat the eggs in a large bowl. Add salt. Once the zucchini is completely cooked, pour in eggs and cover again. Cook until the top is set, or if you are the adventurous type, place a dinner plate on top of the pan and flip the tortilla onto the plate. Slide it back in the pan and cook 3 more minutes, or until the bottom is cooked. Eat as breakfast or as dinner with a side salad, or take it to work as a snack or in the car as a slice on the run.

Fruit and Quinoa Protein Oats

Yield: 1
Prep time: 10 Minutes
Total time: 10 Minutes

A healthy take on overnight oats packed with fruit, protein, and quinoa that are gluten free, dairy free, and vegan!

Ingredients
- 1/4 cup large flaked gluten free rolled oats
- 1/4 cup cooked quinoa
- 2 tablespoons natural vanilla vegan protein powder
- 1 tablespoon ground flaxseed
- 1 tbsp cinnamon
- 1/4 banana, mashed
- A few drops of liquid stevia (or 1 teaspoon pure honey or maple syrup)
- 1/4 cup raspberries
- 1/4 cup blueberries
- 1/4 cup diced peaches
- 3/4 cup unsweetened almond milk
- Optional Toppings: toasted coconut, almond butter, almonds, seeds, dried fruits, fresh fruits, etc.

Directions

In a medium bowl combine oats, quinoa, protein powder, ground flax, cinnamon, and stir to combine

Add in mashed banana, stevia (or honey/maple syrup), berries, and peaches.

Pour in almond milk, and mix ingredients together.

Place in the fridge and leave overnight.

In the morning, remove from the fridge, heat on the stove top or in the microwave, or enjoy cold!

If you find the mixture is too thick in the morning just add in some extra almond milk!

Get creative with toppings... add nut butter, nuts, seeds, more fruit, coconut, etc!

Nutrition

CALORIES: 290
TOTAL FAT: 6g
CARBOHYDRATES: 41g
FIBER: 11g
PROTEIN: 19g

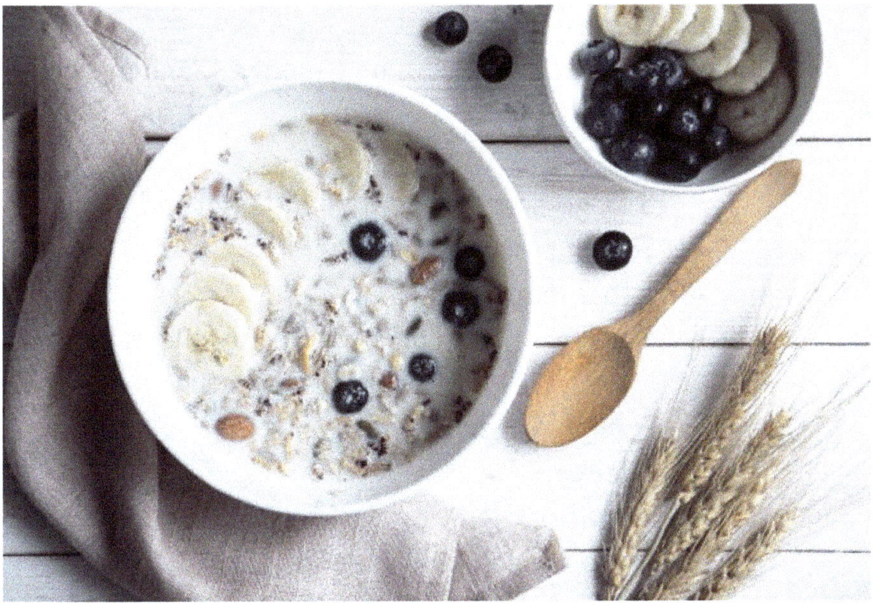

Yogic Carrot Juice

You can use a juicer or a high-speed blender for this recipe.

- 3 large carrots, peeled and chopped
- ¼-inch piece ginger, peeled
- 1 to 2 mint leaves
- Juice or blend carrots, ginger, and mint leaves. Drink at room temperature.
- Lemon Water Delight
- ½ lemon
- 8 ounces room temperature water
- ½ tablespoon baking soda

Squeeze lemon into a glass. Add water and baking soda and stir.

Blueberry & Greek Yogurt Muffins

Yield: 6 Muffins
Prep time: 5 Minutes
Cook time: 18 Minutes
Total time: 23 Minutes

These whole grain muffins are an easy grab-and-go breakfast or snack that will keep you nice & full!

Ingredients

- 1/3c white flour + 1 tbsp (reserved)
- 1/3 c wheat flour
- 2/3 cup protein powder
- 1/2 tbsp baking powder
- 1/4 tbsp salt
- 1/2 cup plain whole milk Greek yogurt
- 1 egg
- 1/2 cup applesauce
- 1/3 cup sugar
- 1 tbsp vanilla
- 1 cup blueberries, fresh or frozen (See notes for frozen)

Directions

Preheat oven to 400 degrees. Line a muffin tin with liners or use non-stick spray.

In a large bowl combine flours, protein powder, baking powder and salt.

In a medium sized bowl whisk together yogurt, egg, applesauce, sugar and vanilla.

Add wet ingredients to the flour mixture and mix until just combined.

Place blueberries in a small bowl and coat with reserved 1 tbsp flour.
Gently fold blueberries into batter.

Fill the prepared muffin tin, nearly filling each muffin to the top. This should make 6 or so muffins, depending on the size of your muffin tin.

Bake muffins at 400 for 18-20 minutes until golden brown and a toothpick inserted comes out clean.

Nutrition
YIELD: 7 SERVING SIZE: 1
CALORIES: 165

TOTAL FAT: 2g
CARBOHYDRATES: 26g
FIBER: 1gSUGAR: 18g
PROTEIN: 11g

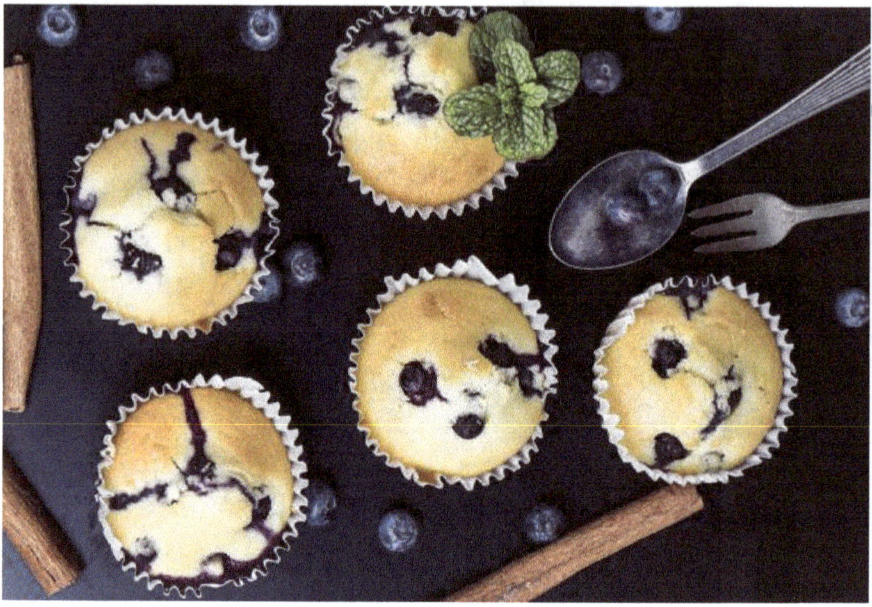

Fruit and Coconut Milk Smoothie

Makes 4 servings

In this smoothie, traditional ingredients like bananas, blueberries, yogurt, and honey meet an unlikely guest: unsweetened coconut milk. Not only does the milk help create the perfect consistency for a smoothie, but it also aids digestion, making this sweet, fruity smoothie a good-for-you treat.

Ingredients

- 1 10-ounce bag frozen blueberries or other fruit
- 3 ripe bananas
- 1 cup plain yogurt
- 1 cup unsweetened coconut milk
- 2 tablespoons honey

How to Make It
In a blender, puree the blueberries, bananas, yogurt, coconut milk, and honey. Serve.

Nutrition

Calories 300

Fat 15g
Carbohydrate 43g
Fiber 3g
Sugars 28g
Protein 5g

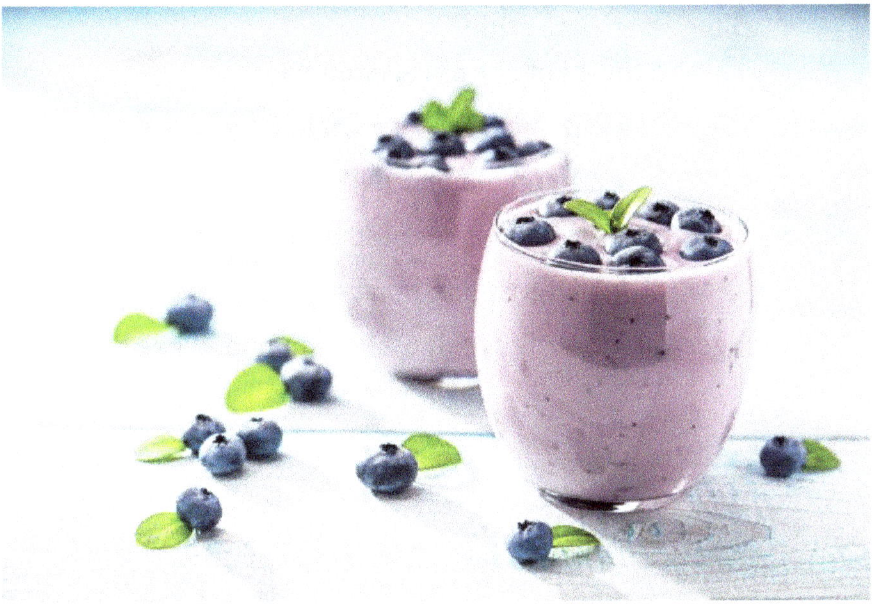

Slumbery Smoothie

This is the perfect afternoon snack.

- 2 cups baby spinach
- 1 cup almond milk
- 1 banana, peeled and sliced
- 1 teaspoon honey

Place all ingredients in a blender and puree.

Success Smoothie

- 1 cup strawberries, sliced
- 1 cup blueberries
- ⅓ banana, sliced
- 1 teaspoon ground flaxseeds
- 1 handful spinach
- 1 teaspoon honey

Blend everything together and enjoy!

Cucumber Chili Coolers

Serves 4-6
Prep Time: 15 minutes
Cook Time: 10 minutes

These edible cups stuffed with a creamy garlic yogurt are so easy to make. Amaze your friends with this delight.

Ingredients

- 2 medium seedless cucumbers, peeled
- 1/2 teaspoon cumin seeds
- 1/2 cup yogurt, whipped
- 1 clove garlic, peeled
- 1 Serrano green chili, seeded
- teaspoon fresh lemon juice
- Table salt, to taste
- sprigs fresh cilantro, stemmed

To make the cucumber cups: Cut the cucumber crosswise into 1-inch pieces. Use a melon baller to scoop out the insides. Leave a 1/4-inch border on the sides and the bottom. Set the cups upside down on a plate lined with paper towels to drain. Refrigerate.

Heat a skillet over medium heat. Add the cumin

seeds and dry roast them until fragrant, about 1 to 2 minutes. Stir constantly to prevent the seeds from burning. Let them cool and then roughly pound them.

Using a hand blender or a mixing spoon, blend together the cumin seeds, yogurt, garlic, green chili, fresh lemon juice, and salt. Transfer the yogurt mixture to a mixing bowl.

Finely chop the cilantro. Add it to the yogurt mixture.

When you are ready to serve, place all the cucumber cups on a serving platter. Spoon the yogurt mix into each cup. These can be made ahead and refrigerated until ready to serve.

Nutrition

Per Serving size: about 1/2 cup
Calories: 50.
Fat: 0g.
Carbohydrates: 12g.
Fiber: 1g.

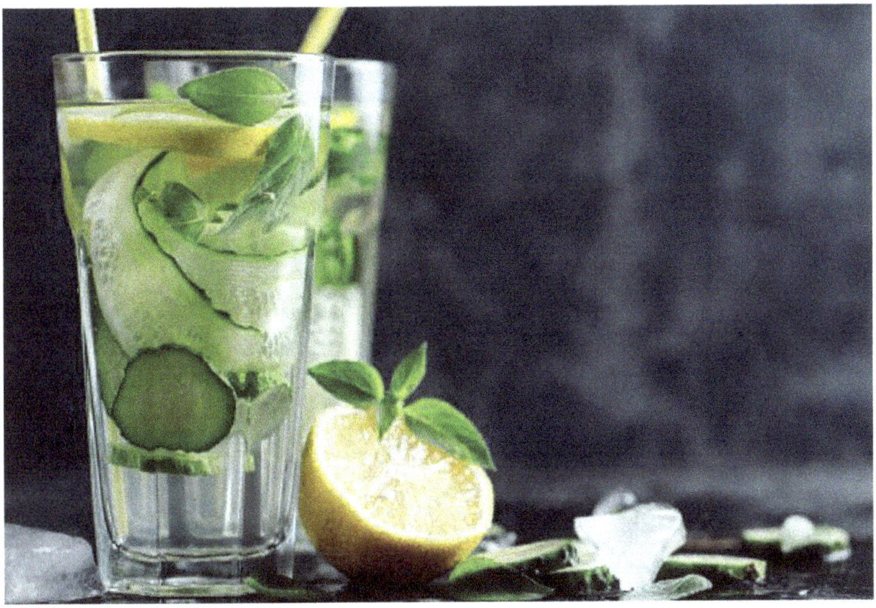

MAIN DISH

Mung Beans & Rice with Vegetables

Ingredients:
- 4 ½ cups water
- ½ cup whole mung beans
- ½ cup basmati rice
- 1 onion, chopped and 3 cloves garlic, minced
- ¾ cup finely minced ginger root
- 3 cups chopped vegetables
- 2 tablespoons ghee or oil
- ¾ tablespoon turmeric
- ¼ teaspoon dried crushed red chilies
- ¼ teaspoon ground black pepper
- ½ teaspoon coriander
- ½ teaspoon cumin
- ½ teaspoon salt

Directions:
Rinse the mung beans and rice. Add the mung beans to boiling water and cook until they begin to split. Add the rice and cook another 15 minutes, stirring occasionally. Now add the vegetables.

Heat the ghee/oil in a sauté pan and add the onions, garlic, and ginger and sauté until clear. Add the spices and cook 5 more minutes, stirring constantly. Add a little water if necessary. Add this to the cooked rice and beans. You can substitute vegetables as you like, as well as use Bragg Liquid Amines, tamari, or soy sauce instead of salt. Tastes great with yogurt!

Nutrition
131 Cal
20g Carbs
4g Fat
4g Protein

Black Eye Bean & Coconut Curry

Ingredients
- ½ cup black eye beans, sprouted if possible
- 2 cups water
- 1 tbsp oil
- 1tbsp mustard seeds
- 1tbsp cumin seeds
- 1 tbsp asafetida
- 1 tbsp grated ginger
- 5-6 curry leaves
- 1 tbsp turmeric
- 1 tbsp coriander powder
- 2 tomatoes - chopped
- 1-2 tbs. roasted peanut powder
- Fresh coriander leaves
- Fresh coconut, grated
- Sugar and salt to taste

Method

Soak the beans in water for 6-8 hours or overnight. Cook the beans in a pressure cooker or boil in a pot.

Heat the oil and add the mustard seeds. When they pop add the cumin seeds, asafetida, ginger, curry leaves, turmeric and coriander powder. Add roasted peanut powder and tomatoes.

Add the beans and water. Continue stirring occasionally until thoroughly cooked.
Add more water if necessary. Add sugar and salt to taste, garnish with coriander leaves and coconut.

Nutrition

200 Calories
13g Carbs
5g Fat
4g Protein

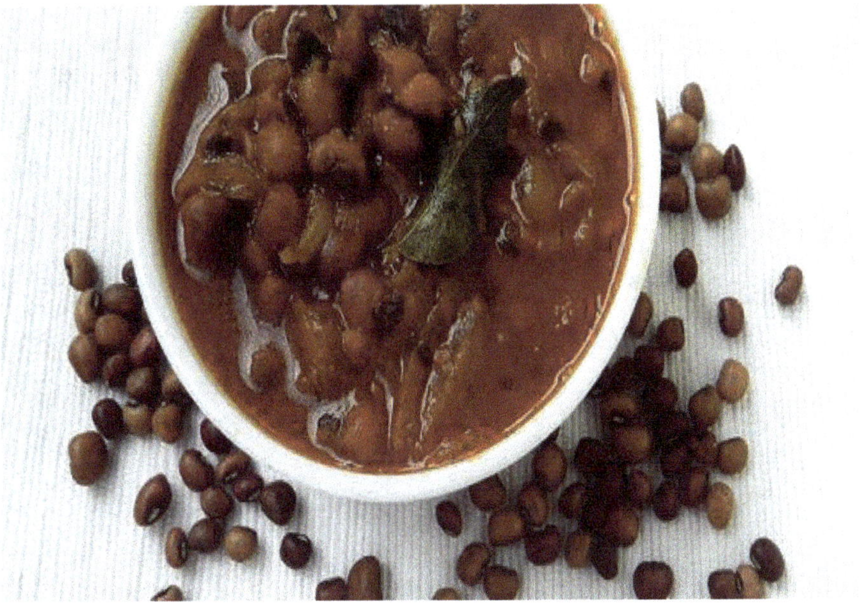

Happiness Salad
- 2 cups baby spinach (or mixture of leafy greens)
- ½ avocado, diced
- 1 cup beets, diced
- ¼ cup hazelnuts
- 2 tablespoons extra virgin olive oil
- 1 tablespoon balsamic vinegar

Put spinach, avocado, beets, and hazelnuts in a bowl. Dress with oil and vinegar. Toss and enjoy.

Peppery-Crusted Tuna
- 1 (5-ounce) piece of wild tuna
- Juice of 1 lemon
- ¼ cup coarsely ground black pepper
- ¼ cup sesame seeds
- 1 tablespoon extra virgin olive oil
- 1 clove garlic, thinly sliced

Put tuna in a bowl and cover in fresh lemon juice. Place pepper and sesame seeds on a flat plate. Dredge tuna in pepper/sesame seeds and coat completely.

Heat oil and garlic in a small pan over high heat. Add tuna to pan and cook 1 minute per side. Serve with a side of sautéed spinach or a side salad dressed with extra virgin olive oil and lemon juice.

Brown Rice Risotto
- 1 tablespoon extra virgin olive oil
- 2 cloves garlic, minced
- 1 large tomato, chopped
- 3 handfuls baby spinach
- 1 cup mushrooms, chopped
- 2 cups broccoli florets
- Salt and pepper, to taste
- 2 cups cooked brown rice
- Pinch saffron
- Grated Parmesan (optional)
- Red chili flakes (optional)

Heat oil in a large skillet over medium heat. Sauté garlic until it just starts to turn golden. Add tomato, spinach, mushrooms, and broccoli. Season with salt and pepper and cook until vegetables are soft. Add rice and saffron and stir, allowing the juice of the vegetables to soak into the rice. Serve warm or cold, sprinkling with Parmesan and/or red pepper flakes, if you like.

Retox Nachos
- 1 tablespoon extra virgin olive oil
- 2 cloves garlic, minced
- 2 cups baby spinach
- ½ pound organic ground beef
- ½ white onion, chopped
- 1 tomato, chopped
- ½ avocado, diced

Sour cream, sliced jalapeños, fresh cilantro, for garnish (optional)
Sesame blue tortilla chips

Heat oil in a pan over medium heat. Add garlic and cook until just turning golden. Add spinach and sauté until wilted, about 5 minutes. Remove from pan and let cool on a plate. In the same pan, add ground beef, breaking it up with a wooden spoon as it cooks. When the meat is cooked through, remove and place on top of the spinach. Top with onion, tomato, and avocado. Garnish with a dollop of sour cream, jalapeños, and cilantro, if desired. Serve with tortilla chips and dive in!

Dome-Free Pasta
- 8 ounces buckwheat pasta
- 1 (14-ounce) can artichoke hearts (in water)
- 1 handful fresh mint
- ½ cup chopped green onion
- 2 tablespoons sunflower seeds (optional)
- 4 tablespoons extra virgin olive oil

Bring a large pot of water to boil. Add pasta and cook 8 to 12 minutes, according to directions on the package. While cooking, chop artichoke hearts and mince the mint. When cooked, drain pasta and put in a bowl. Add artichokes, mint, green onion, and sunflower seeds (if using and you don't suffer from migraines). Drizzle with olive oil and toss. You can serve this hot or cold.

Dome-Soothing Soup
- 1 tablespoon extra virgin olive oil
- 1 yellow onion, diced
- 2 cloves garlic, minced
- 2 (9-ounce) bags baby spinach
- 1 handful fresh mint, roughly chopped
- 2 slices ginger, about the size of a quarter, peeled (optional)
- 1 cup chicken stock (use vegetable stock or water to make this vegetarian)
- 2 pinches salt

Heat the oil in a pot over medium heat. Add onion and garlic and cook until onion is translucent. Be careful not to burn the garlic. Add spinach, mint, and ginger, if using. As the spinach starts to wilt, add stock or water and salt. When the spinach is completely cooked, remove from heat. Blend with an immersion blender, or put in a blender in batches, and puree **until smooth.**

Golden Fish

- 1 tablespoon extra virgin olive oil
- 2 cloves garlic
- 1 large yellow onion, sliced
- 4 (6-ounce) wild caught Alaskan cod (or wild caught fish of choice)
- Juice of 2 lemons
- 1 teaspoon turmeric

Heat oil in a large skillet over medium heat. Add garlic and cook until just starting to turn golden. Add onion and cook until translucent. Squeeze lemon juice over fish and sprinkle with turmeric. Cook fish 5 minutes per side or until it easily flakes with a fork. Serve with a side of rice and vegetables.

Salmon Crush Crunch

- 1 (6-ounce) salmon fillet
- 3 teaspoons olive oil, divided
- 2 cups baby spinach
- 1 cup diced broccoli
- 1 cup cooked quinoa or wild rice
- 1 teaspoon flaxseeds or sesame seeds (optional)

Rub salmon with 1 teaspoon of olive oil. Heat a skillet over medium heat. Add salmon and raise heat to high. Cook for 3 minutes, then turn and cook for another 4 or 5 minutes, until it is cooked through and flakes easily with a fork. Set aside. In the same pan, heat the remaining 2 teaspoons olive oil over medium heat. Add spinach and broccoli and cook until spinach is wilted and broccoli is tender. Add quinoa or rice and mix together. Sprinkle in flax or sesame seeds, if using. Add salmon to pan and flake it with a fork. Stir everything together and serve in a bowl or over a bed of lettuce.

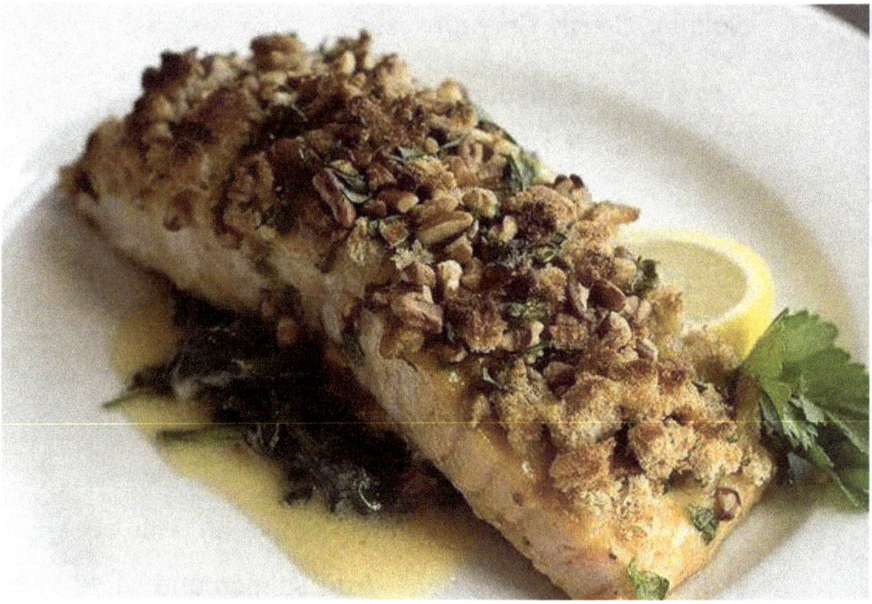

Quinoa Tabouli

I use this as a snack or lunch, and often double the quantities and make as one batch for the week, even using it as garnish on a larger salad or meal.

- ½ cup cooked quinoa
- 2 bunches parsley, finely chopped
- ½ white onion, diced
- 1 tomato, diced
- 1 tablespoon extra-virgin olive oil
- Juice of 1 lemon

Mix the quinoa, parsley, onion, and tomato in a bowl. Dress with olive oil and lemon juice. Stir and enjoy.

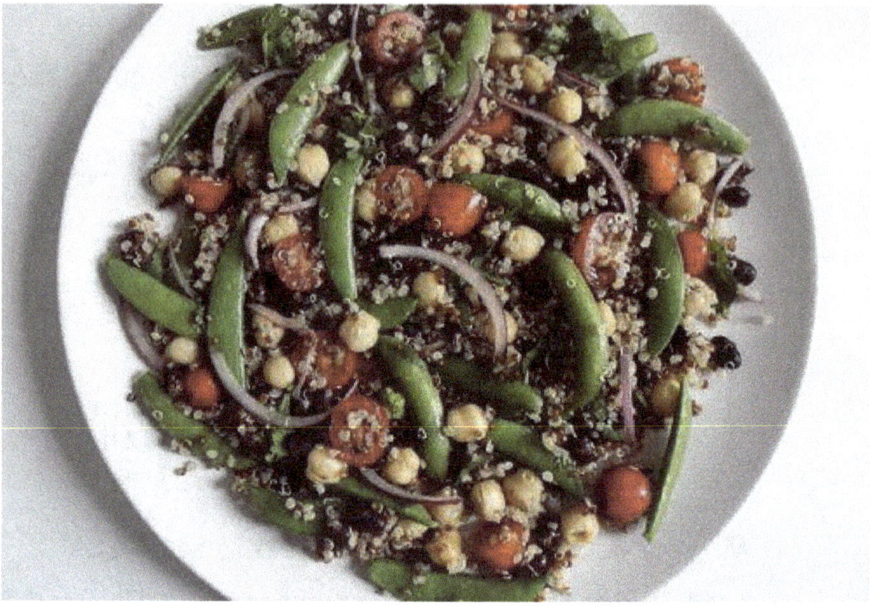

Puffed Millet, Rice & Pomegranate

Ingredients
- 2 cups thin pohe (flattened rice)
- 1 cup puffed millet or rice
- 1 cup thick buttermilk (very thin yogurt)
- 1/2 cup pomegranate pieces
- 5 - 6 curry leaves
- 1/2 teaspoon mustard seeds
- 1/2 teaspoon cumin seeds
- 1/8 teaspoon asafetida
- 5 teaspoons oil
- Sugar to taste
- Salt to taste
- Fresh or dried coconut - shredded
- Fresh coriander leaves

Directions
Heat oil and add mustard seeds.

When they pop add the cumin seeds, asafetida and curry leaves.

In a large bowl place the pohe. Combine it with the oil spice mix, sugar and salt.

When it has cooled mix the yogurt, coriander and coconut with the pohe.

Serve with coriander and coconut if desired.

Nutrition
Calories: 334kcal
Carbohydrates: 23g
Protein: 5g
Fat: 26g
Fiber: 5g

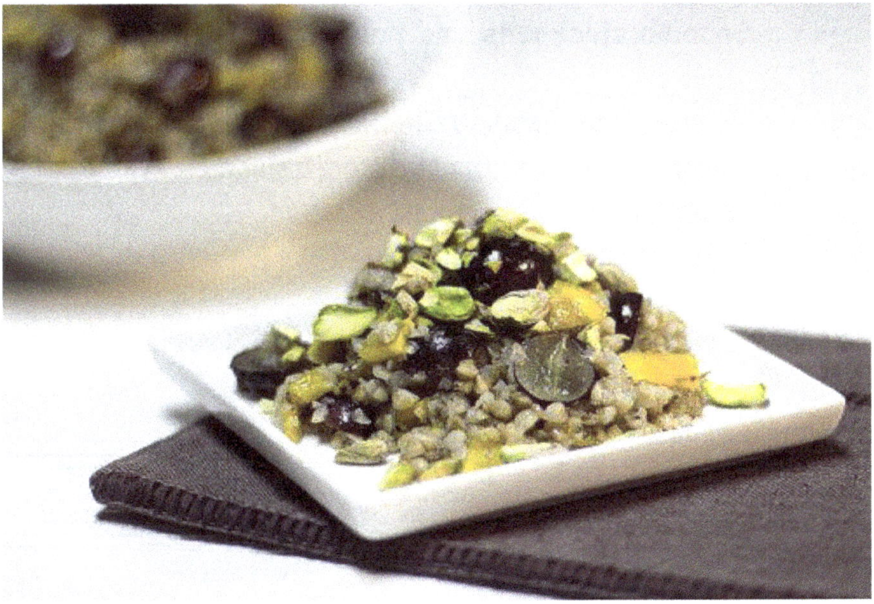

Spanish chickpeas and pasta

This one pot Spanish Chickpeas and pasta has big flavor thanks to liberal dose of spices, artichoke hearts, and fresh lemon.
Prep Time: 10 minutes
Cook Time: 40 minutes
Total Time: 50 minutes

Servings: 4

INGREDIENTS
- 2 Tbsp olive oil
- 2 cloves garlic
- 1/2 Tbsp smoked paprika
- 1 tbsp ground cumin
- 1/2 tbsp dried oregano
- 1/4 tbsp cayenne pepper
- Freshly cracked black pepper
- 1 yellow onion
- 2 cups uncooked vegan pasta
- 1 15oz. can diced tomatoes
- 1 15oz. can quartered artichoke hearts
- 1 19oz. can chickpeas
- 1.5 cups vegetable broth
- 1/2 tbsp salt (or to taste)
- 1/4 bunch fresh parsley
- 1 fresh lemon

DIRECTIONS

Mince the garlic and add it to a large deep skillet along with the olive oil. Cook over medium-low heat for 1-2 minutes, or just until soft and fragrant. Add the smoked paprika, cumin, oregano, cayenne pepper, and some freshly cracked black pepper to the skillet. Stir and sauté the spices in the hot oil for one more minute.

Dice the onion and add it to the skillet. Sauté the onion until it is soft and translucent (about 5 min). Add the pasta and sauté for 2 minutes more.

Drain the chickpeas and artichoke hearts, then add them to the skillet along with the can of diced tomatoes (with juices), vegetable broth, and a half teaspoon of salt. Roughly chop the parsley and add it to the skillet, reserving a small amount to sprinkle over the finished dish. Stir all the ingredients in the skillet until evenly combined.

Place a lid on the skillet and turn the heat up to medium-high. Allow the skillet to come to a boil. Once it reaches a boil, turn the heat down to low and let simmer for 20 minutes. Make sure it's simmering the whole time and adjust the heat up slightly if necessary to keep it simmering.

After simmering for 20 minutes, turn the heat off and let it rest for 5 minutes without removing the lid. Finally, remove the lid, fluff with a fork and top with the remaining chopped parsley. Cut the lemon into wedges and squeeze the fresh juice over each bowl.

NUTRITION
Serving: 1 Serving
Calories: 486.25kcal
Carbohydrates: 83.03g
Protein: 16.08g
Fat: 10.98g
Fiber: 15.28g

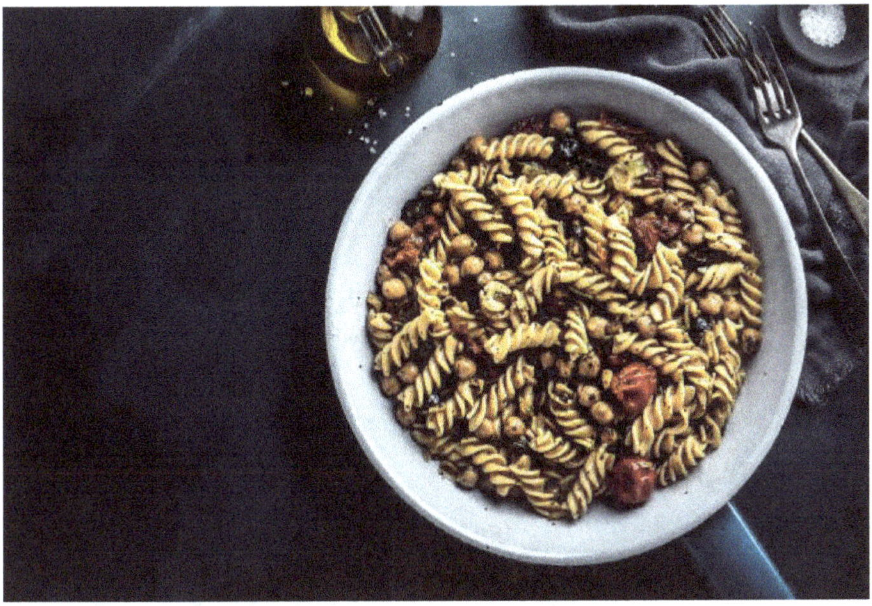

Tamarind Fish Curry

Serves 4
Prep Time: 15 minutes
Cook Time: 35 minutes

If you do not have tamarind, add a bit of lemon juice for a flavor that is similar. Serve with Simple Basmati Rice

Ingredients

- 11/2 pounds, whitefish, cut into chunks
- 3/4 teaspoon and 1/2 teaspoon turmeric powder
- 2 teaspoons tamarind pulp, soaked in 1/4 cup hot water for 10 minutes
- 3 tablespoons vegetable oil
- 1/2 teaspoon black mustard seeds
- 1/4 teaspoon fenugreek seeds
- 8 fresh curry leaves
- large onion, minced
- Serrano green chilies, seeded and minced
- small tomatoes, chopped
- 2 dried red chilies, roughly pounded
- 1 teaspoon coriander seeds, roughly pounded
- 1/2 cup unsweetened desiccated coconut
- Table salt, to taste
- 1 cup water

Directions

Place the fish in a bowl. Rub well with the 3/4 teaspoon turmeric and set aside for about 10 minutes. Rinse and pat dry.

Strain the tamarind and set the liquid aside. Discard the residue.

In a large skillet, heat the vegetable oil. Add the mustard seeds and fenugreek seeds. When they begin to sputter, add the curry leaves, onions, and green chilies. Sauté for 7 to 8 minutes or until the onions are well browned.

Add the tomatoes and cook for another 8 minutes or until the oil begins to separate from the sides of the mixture. Add the remaining 1/2 teaspoon turmeric, the red chilies, coriander seeds, coconut, and salt; mix well, and cook for another 30 seconds.

Add the water and the strained tamarind; bring to a boil. Lower the heat and add the fish. Cook on low heat for 10 to 15 minutes or until the fish is completely cooked. Serve hot.

Nutrition

Calories: 287.
Fat: 0.7g.

Carbohydrates: 75g.
Fiber: 6.1g.
Protein: 3.4g.

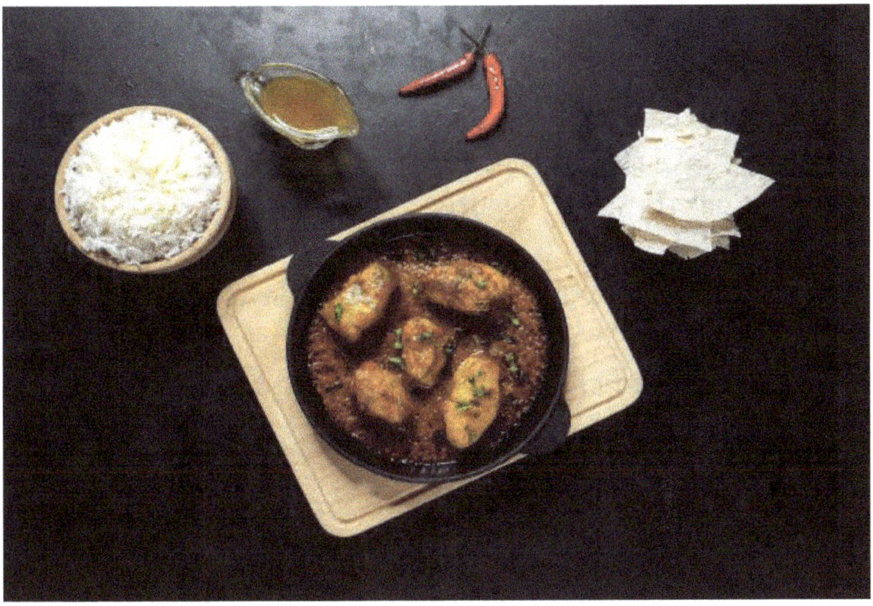

Chili Scallops in Coconut Milk

Serves 4
Prep Time: 10 minutes
Cook Time: 25 minutes

Red chili sambal brings a fiery flavor to the scallops. If you do not have sambal, grind a few dried red chilies along with some water.

Ingredients

- 1 pound sea scallops (or cubed whitefish of your choice)
- 1 tablespoon red chili sambal
- 3 tablespoons vegetable oil
- 1/2 teaspoon mustard seeds
- 8 fresh curry leaves
- 2 teaspoons Ginger-Garlic Paste
- 2 small tomatoes, chopped
- 1/2 teaspoon turmeric powder
- Table salt, to taste
- Water, as needed
- Coconut milk, for garnish

Directions

In a bowl, combine the scallops and the sambal. (If you are using dried red chilies instead, add 2 teaspoons of oil as well.) Set aside for 15 minutes.

While the scallops are marinating, heat the vegetable oil in a medium-sized skillet. Add the mustard seeds; when they begin to sputter, add the curry leaves, ginger paste, and tomatoes. Sauté for about 8 minutes or until the oil begins to separate from the sides of the mixture. Add the turmeric and salt and stir well. Add about 1 cup of water and cook, uncovered, for 10 minutes. Add the scallops (along with all the red chili sambal) and cook on medium heat until the scallops are cooked through, about 5 minutes. Garnish with the coconut milk and serve hot.

Nutrition
Calories 309.3

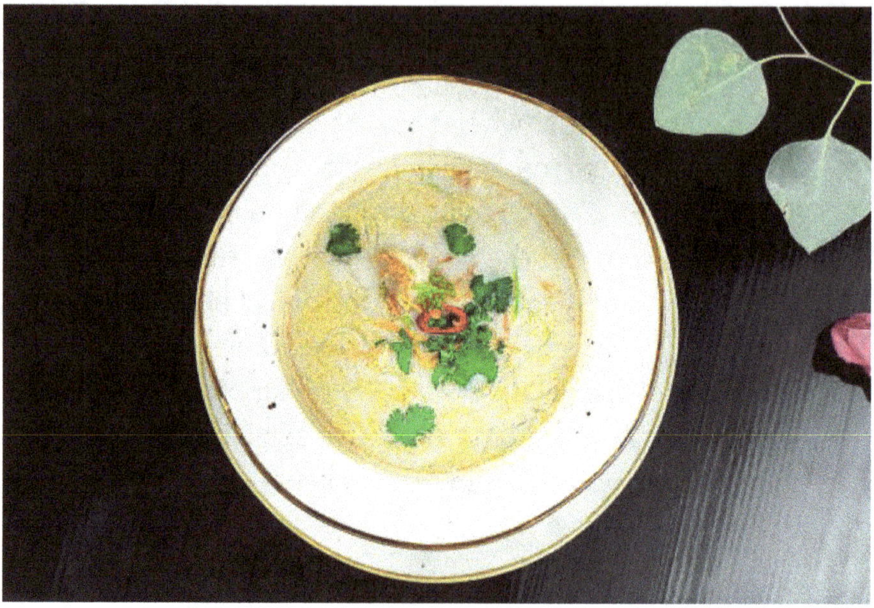

Okra Curry

Ingredients
- 250g okra (ladies finger) – cut into one cm pieces
- 2 tbsp grated ginger
- 1 tbsp mustard seeds
- 1/2 tbsp cumin seeds
- 2 tbsp oil
- Salt to taste
- Pinch asafetida
- 2-3 tbsp roasted peanut powder
- Coriander leaves

Directions
Heat the oil and add the mustard seeds. When they pop add cumin, asafetida and ginger. Cook for 30 seconds.

Add the okra and salt and stir until cooked. Add the peanut powder, cook for another 30 seconds.

Serve with coriander leaves.

Nutrition

Per 1 cup (253ggrams)
Calories 137
Total Fat 8.4ggrams
Total Carbohydrates 15ggrams

Dietary Fiber 5.6ggrams
Protein 3.9g

Vegetable Coconut Curry

Ingredients

- 2 medium sized potatoes r cut in cubes
- 1 1/2 cups cauliflower – cut into florets
- 3 tomatoes r chopped in large pieces
- 1 tbsp oil
- 1 tbsp mustard seeds
- 1 tbsp cumin seeds
- 5-6 curry leaves
- Pinch turmeric - optional
- 1 tbsp grated ginger
- Fresh coriander leaves
- Salt to taste
- Fresh or dried coconut – shredded

Directions

Heat the oil then add the mustard seeds. When they pop add the remaining spices and cook for 30 seconds.

Add the cauliflower, tomato and potato plus a little water, cover and simmer, stirring occasionally until cooked. There should be some liquid remaining. If you want a dry curry then fry for a few minutes until the water has evaporated.

Add coconut, salt and coriander leaves.

Nutrition

Calories 123.8
Total Fat 4.6 g
Total Carbohydrate 18.9 g
Dietary Fiber 5.2 g
Protein 4.3 g

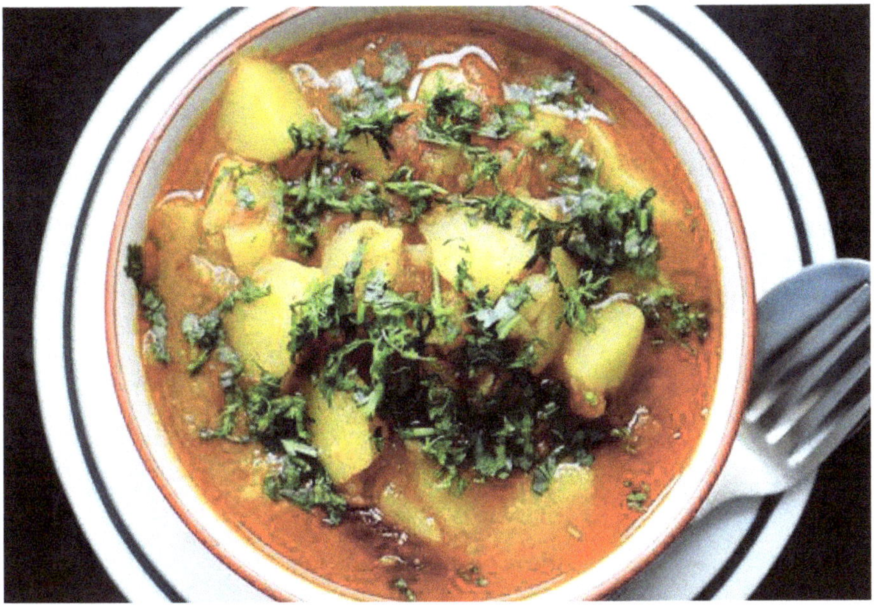

Malabari Chili Fish with Chili Chutney

Serves 4
Prep Time: 15 minutes plus 2 hours to marinate
Cook Time: 20 minutes

Ingredients

- 1 pound whitefish, cut into to 11/2-inch chunks
- 3/4 teaspoon turmeric powder
- Juice of 1/2 lemon
- 1 teaspoon coriander powder
- 1 teaspoon cumin powder
- 1/4 teaspoon black peppercorns, roughly pounded
- 4 dried red chilies, roughly pounded
- Table salt, to taste
- Vegetable oil for deep-frying
- Chaat Spice Mix , optional

Directions

Place the fish cubes in a bowl. Rub them well with the turmeric and set aside for about 10 minutes. Rinse the fish and pat dry.

In a bowl, combine the lemon juice, coriander powder, cumin powder, black pepper, red chilies, and salt; mix well. Add the fish and mix to ensure that all the pieces are well coated. Refrigerate, covered, for 2 hours.

Heat the vegetable oil in a deep fryer or a deep pan to 350°. Deep-fry a few pieces of fish at a time. Remove from the oil with a slotted spoon and drain on a paper towel. Continue until all the fish is fried. Discard any remaining marinade. Serve immediately. Sprinkle Chaat Spice Mix on the fish just prior to serving, if desired.

Nutrition
434 Calories

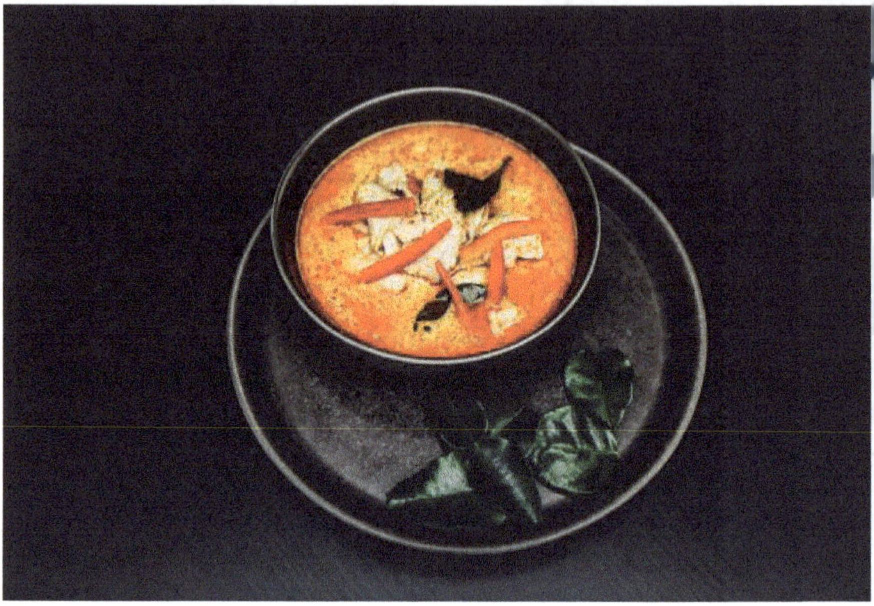

Semolina with Vegetables

Ingredients
- ½ cup semolina
- 1 cup water
- 2 tbsp oil
- 1/4 tbsp mustard seeds
- 1/4 tbsp cumin seeds
- 1 pinch asafetida
- 5-6 curry leaves
- ½ tbsp grated ginger
- ½ tbsp coriander powder
- ½ tbsp cumin powder
- Salt to taste
- 1-2 tomatoes - can cook or eat raw on the side
- 1 cup potatoes, cabbage, cauliflower, carrots, etc.
- Fresh coconut
- Fresh coriander leaves

Directions

Dry roast the semolina in a pan for 10 to 15 minutes till it turns pinkish brown. Remove from the pan.

Heat the oil and add the mustard seeds. When they pop add the cumin, asafetida, curry leaves, ginger, coriander powder and cumin powder. Add vegetables and half cook.

Add the roasted semolina, salt and water. Bring to boil, cover and simmer for 10 minutes. Uncover and fry for 2 to 3 minutes. Add fresh coconut to taste and coriander leaves.

Nutrition
Calories: 231.1
Total Carbohydrate: 42.3 g
Protein: 7.7 g
Total Fat: 3.4 g

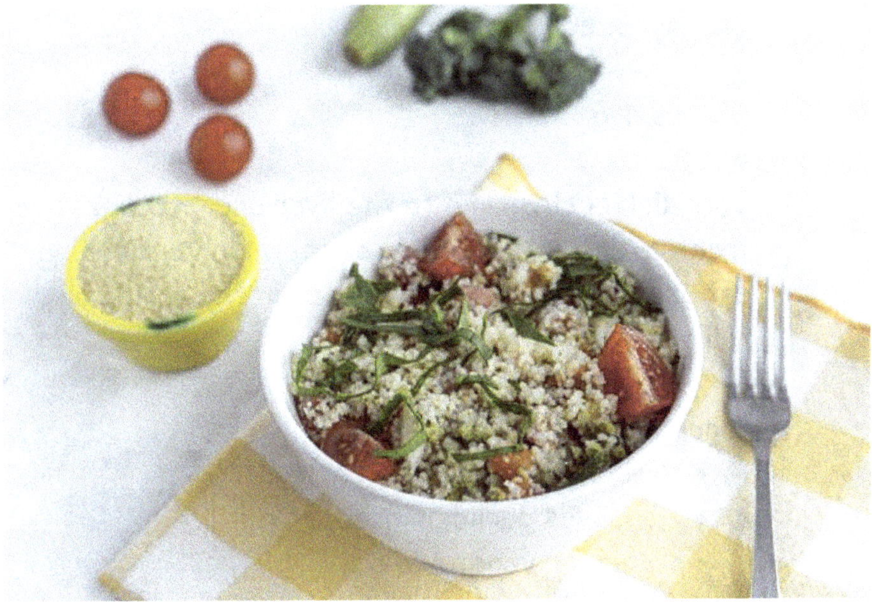

Cheesy Beet-Carrot Casserole

Serves 4-6

This dish is cleansing to the liver and the digestive tract. To help your body do its own inner cleaning, eat as a mono diet for one week in the spring or fall.

Ingredients:
- 2 bunches scallions, chopped
- 3 cloves garlic, minced
- Ghee or vegetable oil
- 1 bunch beets
- 1 lb. carrots
- Soy sauce or Tamari Ground black pepper
- 1 lb. grated cheese

Directions:
Scrub beets and carrots. Steam beets whole. Don't cut off roots or stems. After about 15-20 minutes, add carrots. Steam until tender but firm. Then remove outer peels from beets and carrots. Grate using a coarse grater. Keep beets and carrots separate to preserve their distinct colors.

Sauté scallions and garlic in oil or ghee until tender. Toss with beets and carrots and black pepper. Place in a casserole dish. Sprinkle with Soy sauce or Tamari. Cover with grated cheese and broil until cheese is melted and golden.

Nutrition
Calories 71.9
Total Fat 1.5 g
Total Carbohydrate 13.2 g
Dietary Fiber 3.8 g
Protein 1.8 g

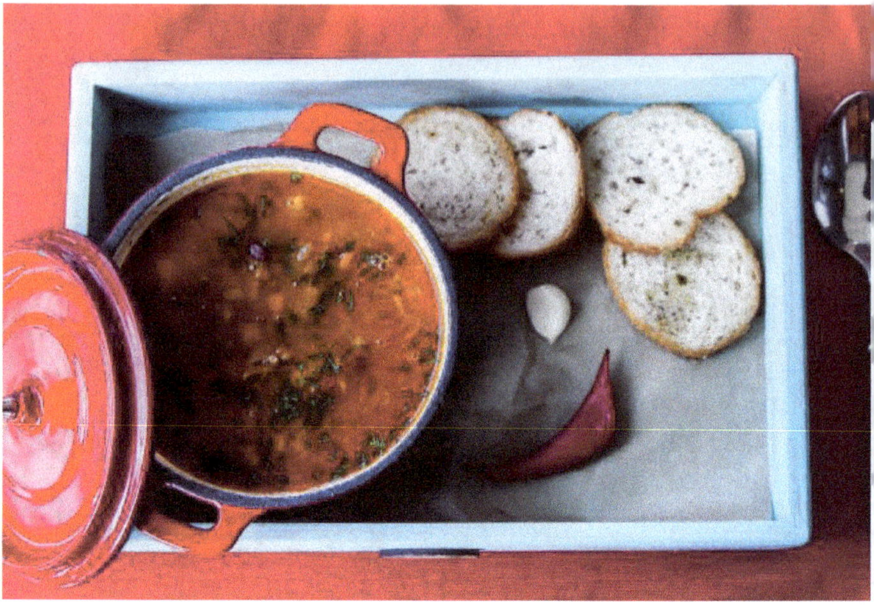

Pumpkin Curry with spicy seeds

Ingredients
- 3 cups pumpkin - chopped in 1-2 cm pieces
- 2 tbsp oil
- ½ tbsp mustard seeds
- ½ tbsp cumin seeds
- Pinch asafetida
- 5-6 curry leaves
- ¼ tbsp fenugreek seeds
- 1/4 tbsp fennel seeds
- 1/2 tbsp grated ginger
- 2 inch piece dry tamarind fruit (soaked in hot water) or 1 tbsp tamarind paste
- 2 Tbsp - dry, ground coconut
- 2 Tbsp roasted ground peanut
- Salt and brown sugar or jaggery to taste
- Fresh coriander leaves

Directions

Heat the oil and add the mustard seeds. When they pop add the cumin, fenugreek, asafetida, ginger, curry leaves and fennel. Cook for 30 seconds.

Add pumpkin and salt. Add the tamarind paste or water with pulp inside. Add the jaggery or brown sugar. Add ground coconut and peanut powder. Cook for a few more minutes. Add fresh chopped coriander.

Nutrition
Calories 191
Total Fat 11ggrams
Total Carbohydrates 21ggrams
Dietary Fiber 3.7ggrams
Protein 5.3g

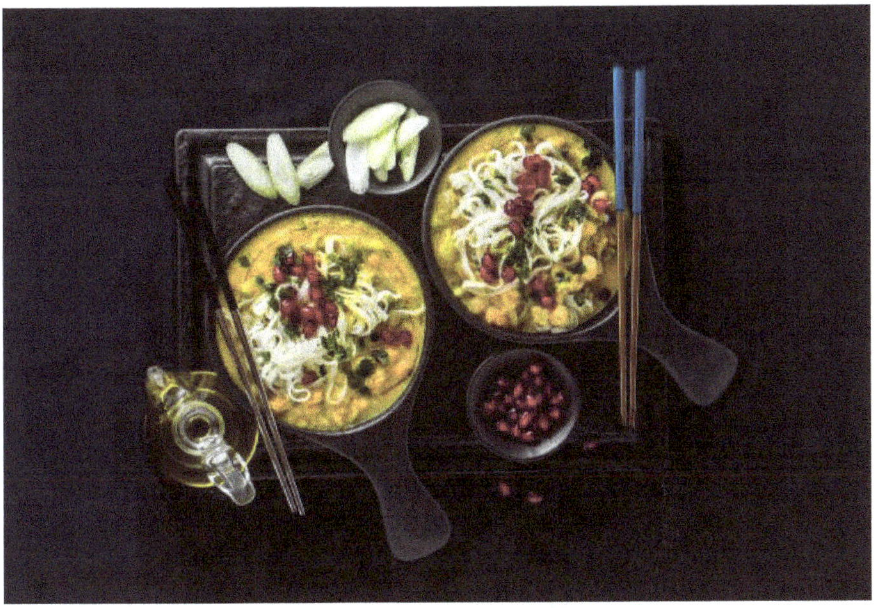

Creamy Almond Chicken

Serves 4-5
Prep Time: 10 minutes
Cook Time: 35-40 minutes

The nuts add a rich creamy taste to the chicken. Serve this with the Carom-Flavored Flatbread

Ingredients
- 1/4 cup blanched almonds
- Water, as needed
- 4 tablespoons vegetable oil
- bay leaf
- cloves
- 5 peppercorns
- 1 green chili, seeded and minced
- 1 tablespoon Ginger-Garlic Paste
- 8 pieces skinless, bone-in chicken thighs
- 1/2 teaspoon red chili powder
- 1/4 teaspoon turmeric powder
- 1 teaspoon coriander powder
- 1/2 teaspoon Warm Spice Mix
- Table salt, to taste
- 1/4 cup plain yogurt, whipped
- 1/4 cup heavy cream

Directions
In a blender or food processor, blend the almonds with a few tablespoons of water to make a thick,

smooth paste. Set aside. In a large pan, heat the vegetable oil on medium. Add the bay leaf, cloves, peppercorns, green chili, and Ginger-Garlic Paste; sauté for about 10 seconds. Add the chicken and sauté until well browned on both sides, about 5 to 10 minutes.

Add the red chili, turmeric, coriander, the spice mix, and salt; cook for about 5 minutes. Add the yogurt and sauté until the fat begins to separate. Add about 1/2 cup of water. Cover and simmer until the chicken is tender and cooked through, about 10 to 15 minutes. Stir occasionally, adding a few tablespoons of water if the dish seems too dry. Add the almond paste and the cream. Cook, uncovered, on medium heat for about 8 minutes.

Serve hot.

Nutrition

535 Cal
60g Carbs
22g Fat
50g Protein

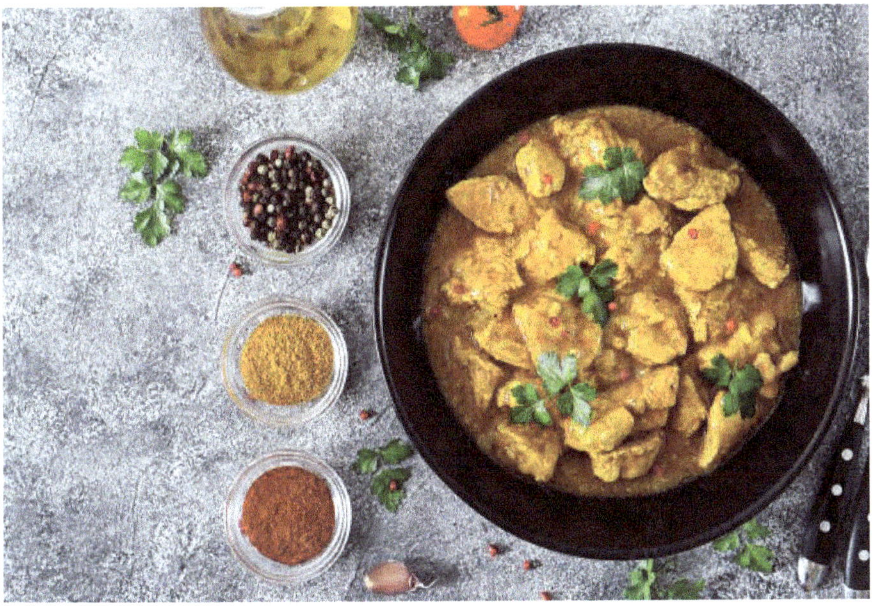

Hot Spiced Lamb

Serves 4
Prep Time: 10 minutes
Cook Time: 1 hour

Ingredients
- 1 1/4 pounds lean minced lamb
- 1 teaspoon grated fresh gingerroot
- 1/2 teaspoon red chili powder
- teaspoon minced garlic
- tablespoons plain yogurt, whipped
- 1/4 teaspoon turmeric powder
- 1 Serrano green chili, seeded and minced
- 1/2 cup water
- tablespoons vegetable oil
- 1 large red onion, minced
- 1/4 cup unsweetened desiccated coconut
- Table salt, to taste
- 1/2 teaspoon Warm Spice Mix

Directions

In a deep pan, combine the lamb, ginger, red chili powder, garlic, yogurt, turmeric, and green chili. Add the water and bring to a boil. Cover and simmer over low heat for about 45 minutes or until the lamb is cooked through. Set aside.

In a large skillet, heat the vegetable oil. Add the

onion and fry, stirring constantly, until well browned, about 8 minutes. Add the lamb and fry for another 4 to 5 minutes. Add the coconut and salt; sauté for another 5 minutes. Serve hot, garnished with Warm Spice Mix.

Nutrition

294 calories

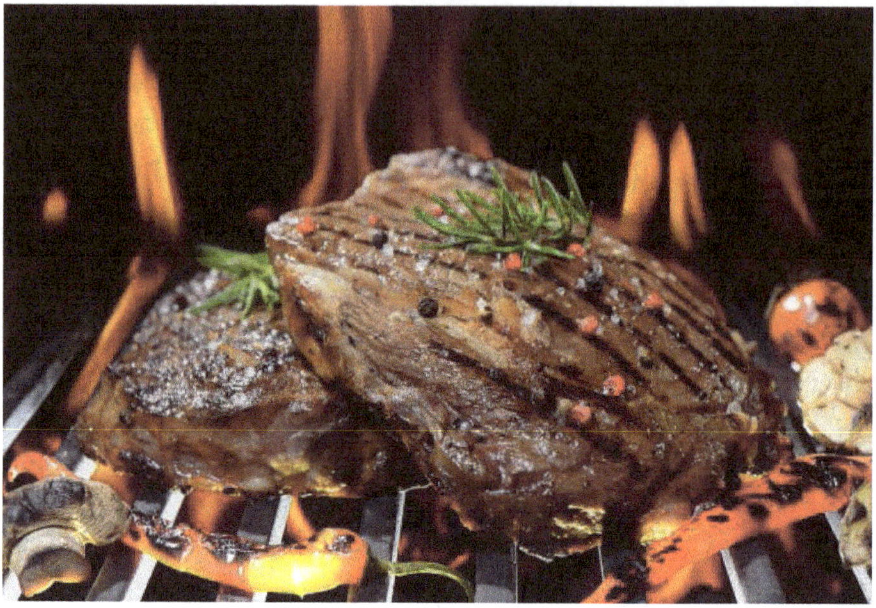

Lobster Thermidor in Nutty Sauce

Serves 4
Prep Time: 15 minutes
Cook Time: 20 minutes

Keep the lobster shell and spoon the dish into the shell for a lovely presentation.

Ingredients

- 3 tablespoons unsalted cashew nuts, soaked in water for 10 minutes
- 2 tablespoons white poppy seeds, soaked in water for
- 20 minutes
- Water, as needed
- 2 tablespoons blanched almonds
- 2 teaspoons white sesame seeds
- 3 tablespoons Clarified Butter
- 1 (1-inch) cinnamon stick
- 1 black cardamom pod, bruised
- small bay leaf
- cloves
- 1 green cardamom pod, bruised
- teaspoon Ginger-Garlic Paste
- Serrano green chilies, seeded and minced
- 1/2 teaspoon red chili powder
- 1/4 teaspoon turmeric powder
- 1 cup yogurt, whipped

- 1 1/2 pounds cooked lobster meat
- Table salt, to taste
- 1 teaspoon Warm Spice Mix

Directions

Drain the cashews and poppy seeds and process or blend together with the almonds and sesame seeds using just enough water to make a thick paste. Set aside.

In a large skillet, heat the butter. Add the cinnamon stick, black cardamom pod, bay leaf, cloves, and green cardamom pod. When the spices begin to sizzle, add the Ginger-Garlic Paste, green chilies, and the nut paste. It will splatter a little; add 1 tablespoon of water to stop the splattering. Fry, stirring constantly, until the oil begins to separate from the mixture.

Add the red chili powder, turmeric, yogurt, lobster, salt, and spice mix. Fry, stirring constantly, until the lobster is heated through. Serve hot.

Nutrition

Calories 280

Total fat 17g
Total carbohydrate 5g,
Dietary fiber 0g
Protein 23g

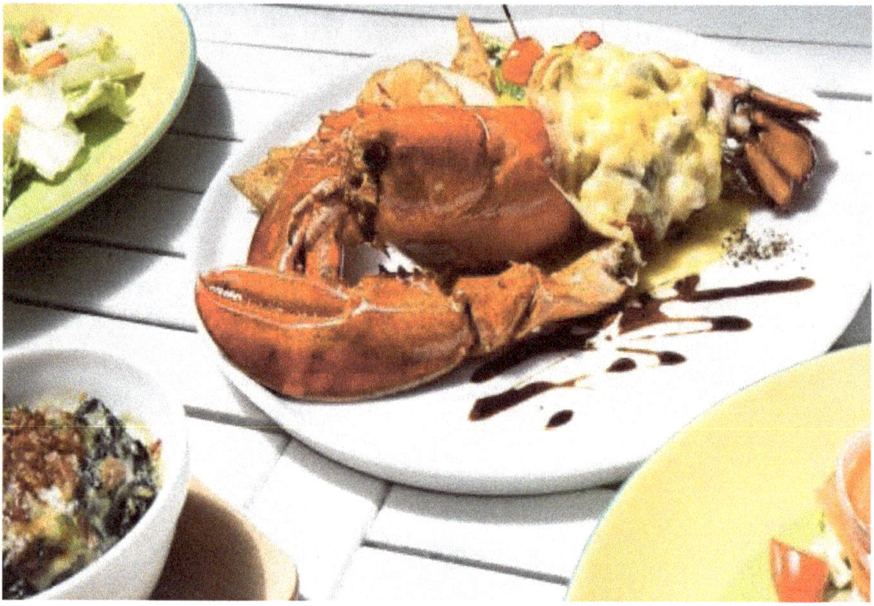

Red Chili Fish Fry

Serves 4
Prep Time: 15 minutes
Cook Time: 20 minutes

Serve with Simple Basmati Rice. For a milder version, add 1/2 cup of light coconut milk instead of water in step 4.

Ingredients
- 4 whitefish filets (such as tilapia, catfish, or cod)
- 3/4 teaspoon turmeric powder
- 3 tablespoons vegetable oil
- 1/2 teaspoon black mustard seeds
- 8 fresh curry leaves
- 4 dried red chilies, roughly pounded
- large onion, minced
- teaspoons Ginger-Garlic Paste
- 1/2 teaspoon red chili powder
- 1/4 teaspoon turmeric powder
- Table salt, to taste
- 1/2 cup water

Directions

Place the fish filets in a bowl. Rub them well with the turmeric and set aside for about 10 minutes. Rinse the filets and pat dry.

In a large skillet, heat the vegetable oil. Add the mustard seeds and when they begin to sputter, add the curry leaves, red chilies, and onions. Sauté for about 6-7 minutes or until well browned. Add the Ginger-Garlic Paste, red chili powder, turmeric powder, and salt; mix well.

Add the fish and fry for 3 minutes. Turn and fry for another 3 minutes. Add 1/2 cup of water and bring to a boil. Cover, lower heat, and simmer for about 6 to 8 minutes or until the fish is completely cooked through. Serve hot.

Calories-432

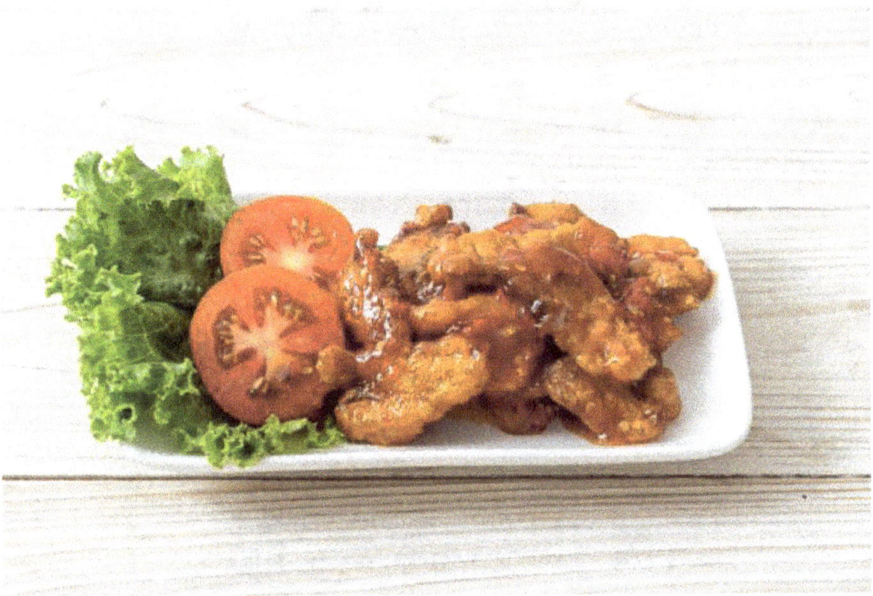

Salmon in Saffron-Flavored Curry

Serves 4
Prep Time: 10 minutes
Cook Time: 10 minutes

Ingredients

- 4 tablespoons vegetable oil
- 1 large onion, finely chopped
- teaspoon Ginger-Garlic Paste
- 1/2 teaspoon red chili powder
- 1/4 teaspoon turmeric powder
- teaspoons coriander powder
- Table salt, to taste
- 1 pound salmon, boned and
- cubed
- 1/2 cup plain yogurt, whipped
- 1 teaspoon Roasted Saffron

Directions

In a large, nonstick skillet, heat the vegetable oil. Add the onions and sauté for 3 to 4 minutes or until transparent. Add the Ginger-Garlic Paste and sauté for 1 minute.

Add the red chili powder, turmeric, coriander, and salt; mix well. Add the salmon and sauté for 3 to 4 minutes. Add the yogurt and lower the heat.

Simmer until the salmon has cooked through. Add the saffron and mix well. Cook for 1 minute. Serve hot.

Nutrition

Calories 400

Fat 26.8 g

Carbohydrate 1.6 g

Fiber 0 g

Protein 33.9 g

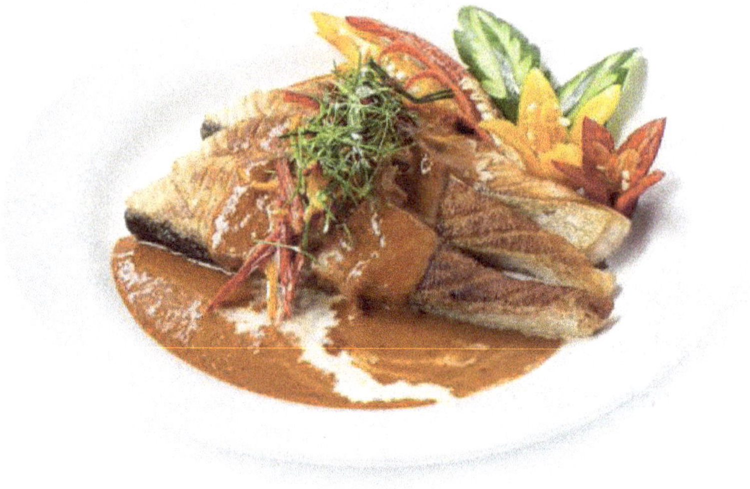

Pork Bafat

Serves 4
Prep Time: 5 minutes
Cook Time: 30-40 minutes

Ingredients
- 1 tablespoon Ginger-Garlic Paste
- 4 black peppercorns
- 4 cloves
- 1 teaspoon cumin seeds
- 1/4 teaspoon black mustard seeds
- 8 dried red chilies
- 1/4 cup malt vinegar
- 4 tablespoons vegetable oil
- 1 pound pork, cubed
- 1 tablespoon tamarind pulp, soaked in 1/4 cup hot water for 10 minutes
- 1 cup frozen pearl onions
- Table salt, to taste
- Water, as needed

Directions

In a food processor, grind together the Ginger-Garlic Paste, black peppercorns, cloves, cumin seeds, mustard seeds, red chilies, and malt vinegar. Set aside.

In a large skillet, heat the vegetable oil; add the

pork and brown on all sides, about 8 to 10 minutes. Add the ground paste and sauté for 10 more minutes.

Strain the tamarind and discard the residue. Add the strained liquid to the pork and mix well. Add the frozen onions and salt; cook, uncovered, for about 5 minutes.

Add 1/2 cup of water. Lower the heat and simmer, uncovered, until the pork is cooked, about 10 to15 minutes. Stir occasionally. Add more water if the dish becomes too dry or starts to stick. Serve hot.

Nutrition
378. Cal 8g Carbs, 22g Fat, 24g Protein

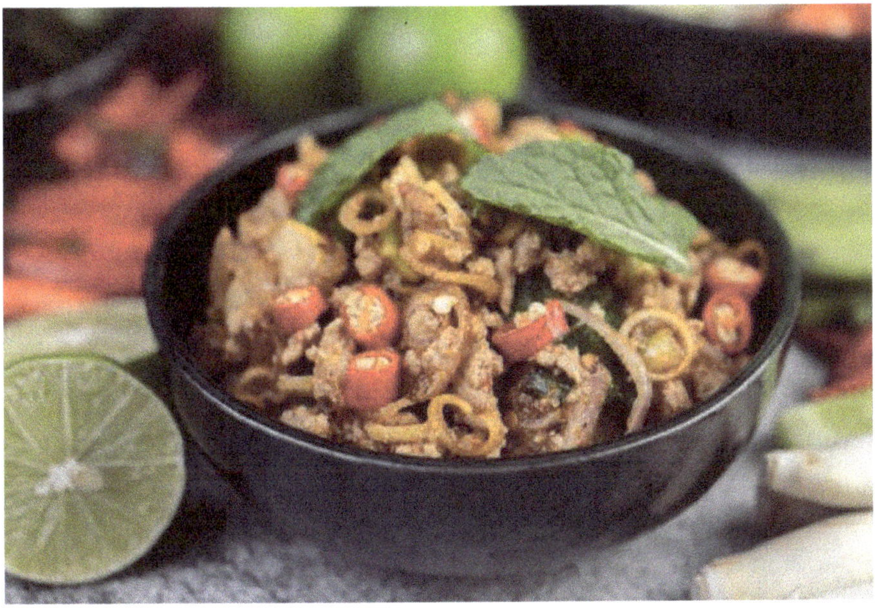

Fish in a Velvety Serrano Sauce

Serves 4
Prep Time: 20 minutes
Cook Time: 30 minutes

Ingredients
- 4-5 catfish filets
- 3/4 teaspoon turmeric powder
- 8 tablespoons vegetable oil, divided
- bay leaf
- 1/2 teaspoon cumin seeds
- teaspoons Ginger-Garlic Paste
- 1 large red onion, minced
- teaspoon red chili powder
- Serrano green chilies, seeded and minced
- 1/2 cup plain yogurt, whipped
- Table salt, to taste
- Water, as needed

Directions
Place the catfish filets in a bowl. Rub the filets well with the turmeric and set aside for about 10 minutes. Rinse the filets and pat dry. In a medium-sized skillet, heat 6 tablespoons of the vegetable oil. Add 1 filet at a time and fry until brown on both sides. Remove from heat with a slotted spoon and drain on a paper towel. Continue until all the filets are fried. Set aside.

In a large skillet, heat the remaining 2 tablespoons of vegetable oil. Add the bay leaf and cumin seeds. When the spices begin to sizzle, add the Ginger-Garlic Paste and onions; sauté for about 7 to 8 minutes or until the onions are well browned.

Add the red chili powder and green chilies; mix well. Add the yogurt and salt, and mix well. Add about 1/2 cup of water. Simmer, uncovered, on low heat for about 10 minutes, stirring constantly

Add the fish filets and simmer for another 5 minutes. Be careful not to break the filets when you stir. Serve hot.

Nutrition

Calories: 205
Total Fat: 13.9 g
Cholesterol: 70 mg
Sodium: 90 mg

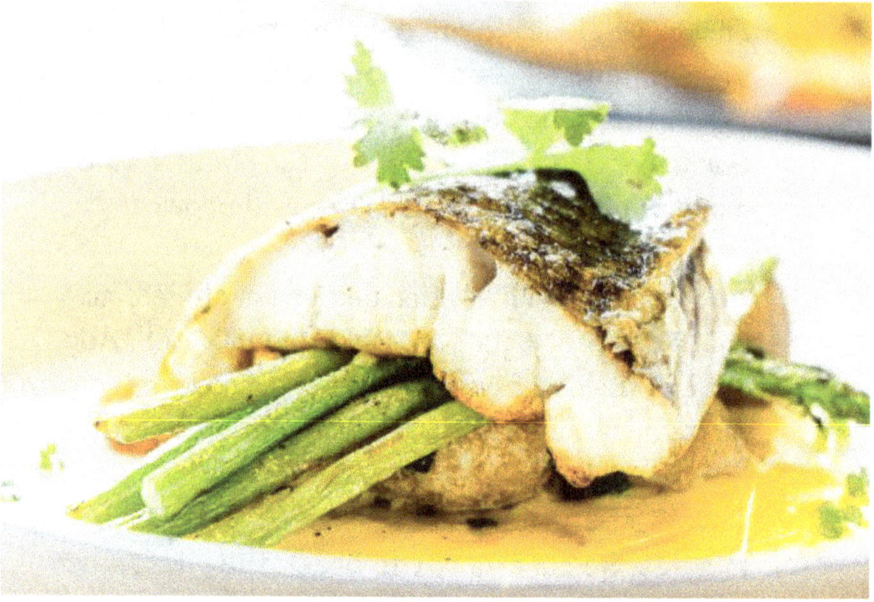

Spicy Shrimp in Coconut Milk

Serves 4
Prep Time: 10 minutes
Cook Time: 20 minutes

A nice variation is to fry the shrimp first. It adds a nice crispness. Serve with steamed white rice.

Ingredients

- 1 bay leaf
- 1 teaspoon cumin seeds
- (1-inch) cinnamon stick
- cloves
- black peppercorns
- 1-inch piece fresh gingerroot, peeled and sliced
- garlic cloves
- Water, as needed
- 3 tablespoons vegetable oil
- 1 large red onion, minced
- 1/2 teaspoon turmeric powder
- 1 pound shrimp, peeled and deveined
- 1 (14-ounce) can light coconut milk
- Table salt, to taste

Directions
In a spice grinder, roughly grind the bay leaf, cumin seeds, cinnamon stick, cloves, peppercorns,

ginger, and garlic. Add 1 tablespoon of water if needed.

In a medium-sized skillet, heat the vegetable oil. Add the ground spice mixture and sauté for about 1 minute. Add the onions and sauté for 7 to 8 minutes or until the onions are well browned.

Add the turmeric and mix well. Add the shrimp and sauté for about 2 to 3 minutes, until no longer pink. Add the coconut milk and salt. Simmer for 10 minutes or until the gravy starts to thicken. Remove from heat and serve hot.

Nutrition
Calories: 757.5
Total Carbohydrate: 14.2 g
Protein: 49.4 g

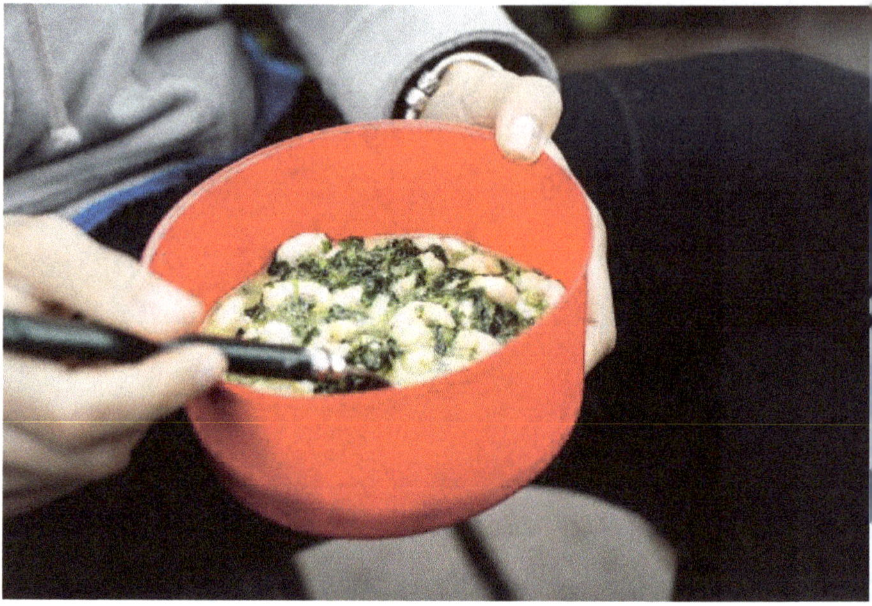

Parsi Fish

Serves 4
Prep Time: 10 minutes
Cook Time: 20-30 minutes

A perfect recipe when you have lots of leftover chutney and very little time.

Ingredients
- 4 (1-inch-thick) fish steaks (your choice of type)
- 3/4 teaspoon turmeric powder
- 8 tablespoons Green Chili
- Coconut Chutney

Directions
Place the fish steaks in a bowl. Rub the steaks well with the turmeric and set aside for about 10 minutes. Rinse and pat dry

Cut 4 squares of aluminum foil large enough to accommodate the steaks. Place a steak in the center of each piece of foil. Cover the fish with 2 generous tablespoons of the chutney. Fold the foil over it as if you were wrapping a present. Leave a little room for the steam to expand.

Preheat the oven to 400°.

Place the foil packages on a baking sheet. Bake until the fish is completely cooked through (20 to25 minutes for 1-inch-thick steaks). The timing will depend on the thickness of your steak. Serve hot.

Nutrition

Servings per Recipe: 3
Calories 1,439.6

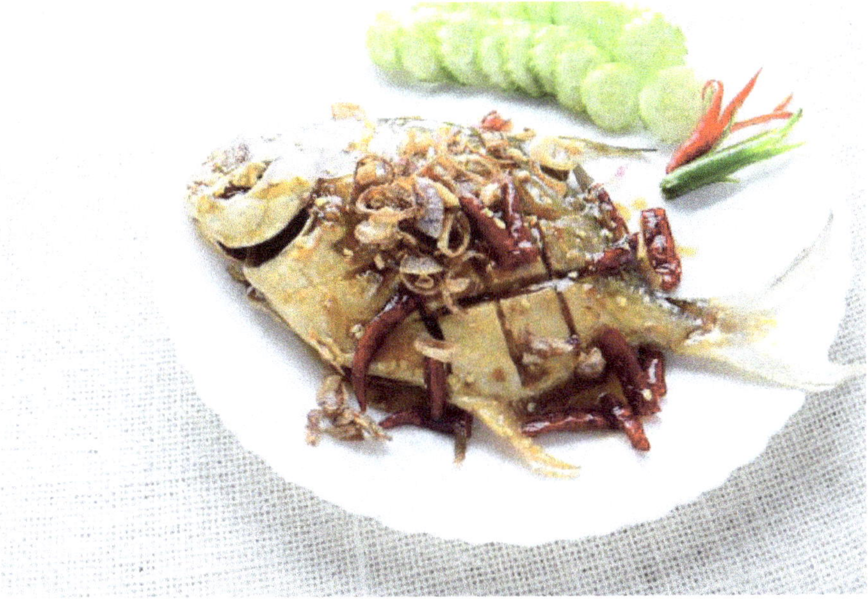

Wasabi Chicken Tikka

Serves 4
Prep Time: 10 minutes
Cook Time: 20 minutes

Ingredients
- 3 tablespoons vegetable oil
- 1 medium-sized red onion, finely chopped
- 1 tablespoon Ginger-Garlic Paste
- 2 medium tomatoes, finely chopped
- 1/2 teaspoon red chili powder
- 1/4 teaspoon turmeric powder
- Table salt, to taste
- 1/2 teaspoon Warm Spice Mix
- 3/4 cup heavy cream.
- 1 recipe Chicken Tikka
- 2 tbsp wasabi sauce

Directions

In a large pan, heat the vegetable oil on medium. Add the onions and sauté until well browned, about 7 to 8 minutes. Add the Ginger-Garlic Paste and sauté for another minute.

Add the tomatoes and cook for about 8 minutes or until the tomatoes are cooked and the oil begins to separate from the sides of the mixture. Add the red chili, turmeric, salt, and the spice mix; sauté for 1 minute.

Stir in wasabi teriyaki sauce

Add the cream and cook for about 2 minutes. Add the Chicken Tikka and mix well. Cook for 2 minutes or until the chicken is heated through. Serve hot.

Nutrition

101 Calories
10g Carbs

Chicken with Nuts in a Creamy Sauce

Ingredients
- 2 small red onions, peeled and chopped
- 1-inch piece fresh gingerroot, peeled and sliced
- 4 garlic cloves, peeled
- 4 dried red chilies
- 2 teaspoons coriander powder
- Water, as needed
- 3 tablespoons unsalted cashew nuts, soaked in water for 10 minutes
- 2 tablespoons white poppy seeds, soaked in water for
- 20 minutes
- 2 tablespoons almonds, blanched
- 3 tablespoons Clarified Butter
- 2 (1-inch) cinnamon sticks
- 2 black cardamom pods, bruised
- 1 large bay leaf
- 2 green cardamom pods, bruised
- 1 teaspoon cumin powder
- 1 cup plain yogurt, whipped
- 11/2 pounds boneless diced chicken
- Table salt, to taste
- 1 teaspoon Warm Spice Mix
- Roasted cumin seeds, for garnish

Directions
In a blender or food processor, blend together the

onions, ginger, garlic, red chilies, coriander powder, and up to 1/4 cup of water to make a paste. Set aside. Process or blend together the cashew nuts, poppy seeds, almonds, and just enough water to make a smooth, thick paste. Set aside.

In a deep pan, heat the Clarified Butter over medium heat. Add the cinnamon sticks, black cardamom, bay leaf, cloves, and green cardamom; sauté until fragrant, about 11/2 minutes. Add the onion paste and cumin. Sauté over medium-low heat, stirring constantly, until the butter separates from the onion paste. Add the yogurt and continue cooking for about 12 minutes, stirring constantly.

Add the chicken pieces. Simmer, covered, for 15 to 20 minutes or until the chicken is tender.

Add the nut paste and simmer, uncovered, for about 4 minutes. Stir in the salt and the Warm Spice Mix.

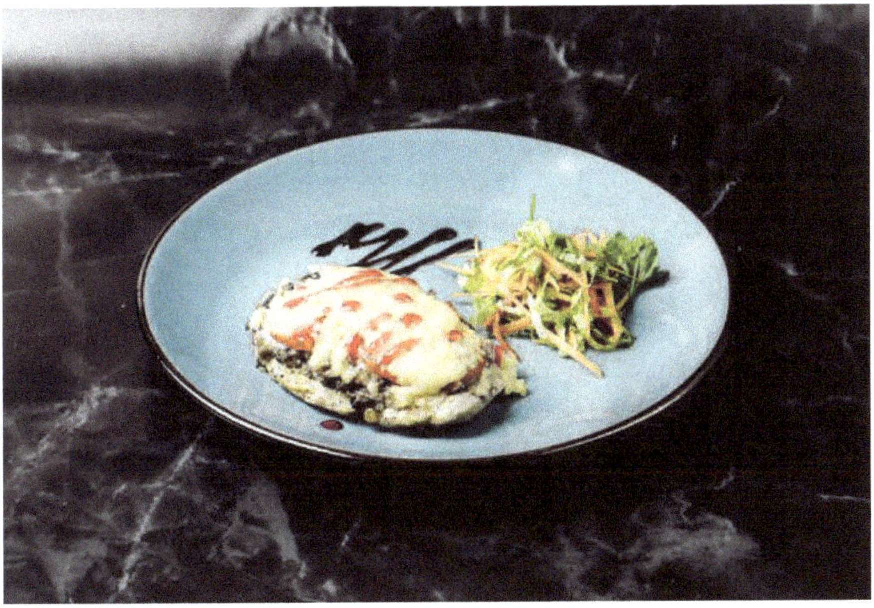

VEGAN CURRIES

Basic Vegetable Curry

- 250gms vegetables – chopped
- 1 tsp oil
- ½ tsp mustard seeds
- ½ tsp cumin seeds
- Pinch asafoetida
- 4-5 curry leaves
- ¼ tsp turmeric
- ½ tsp coriander powder
- Pinch chilli powder
- Grated ginger
- Fresh coriander leaves
- Sugar / jaggery and salt to taste
- Fresh or dried coconut

1. Cut up vegetable into small pieces (1-2 cm) depending on the vegetable.
2. Heat the oil then add the mustard seeds. When they pop add the cumin, ginger and remaining spices.
3. Add the vegetables and cook. At this point you may want to fry the vegetables until they are cooked or add some water, cover the pot and simmer. It will depend on the vegetables being used and individual preference. Cooking time will also vary depending on the vegetables used.
4. When the vegetables are cooked add any sugar, salt, coconut and coriander.

You can vary the spices used depending on your preference – you may increase the chilli, ginger or coriander, or decrease others. There are many other spices that can be added such as ajwain, fennel, aniseed, cinnamon, clove, garam masala, cardamom, tamarind etc. In Maharashtra a few tsps of roasted peanut powder is often used. You can experiment with ground peanut, almond, cashew etc

Any vegetables can be prepared in this way. You can experiment with dry and wet curries, combine vegetables, mash tomatoes as a base with the spicy mix, combine cooked lentils and so on. If you are using more than one vegetable be aware of which vegetables take longer to cook and add them first.

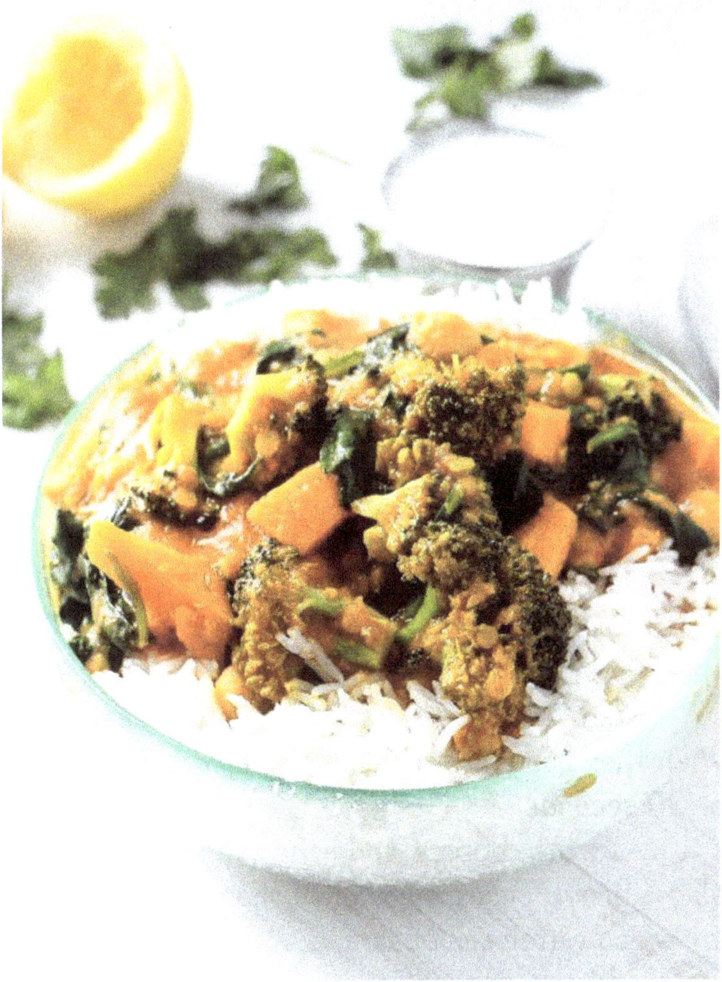

Cabbage Curry

Patta Kobi Bhaji

- 3 cups cabbage - shredded
- 1 tsp oil
- 1 tsp mustard seeds
- 1 tsp cumin seeds
- 4-5 curry leaves
- Pinch turmeric r optional
- 1 tsp grated ginger
- Fresh coriander leaves
- Salt for taste
- Optional - ½ cup green peas, sweet corn or potato to add variety

1. Heat the oil then add the mustard seeds. When they pop add the remaining spices and cook for 30 seconds.
2. Add the cabbage and other vegetables if using, stirring occasionally until thoroughly cooked. If needed water can be added.
3. Add salt to taste and coriander leaves.

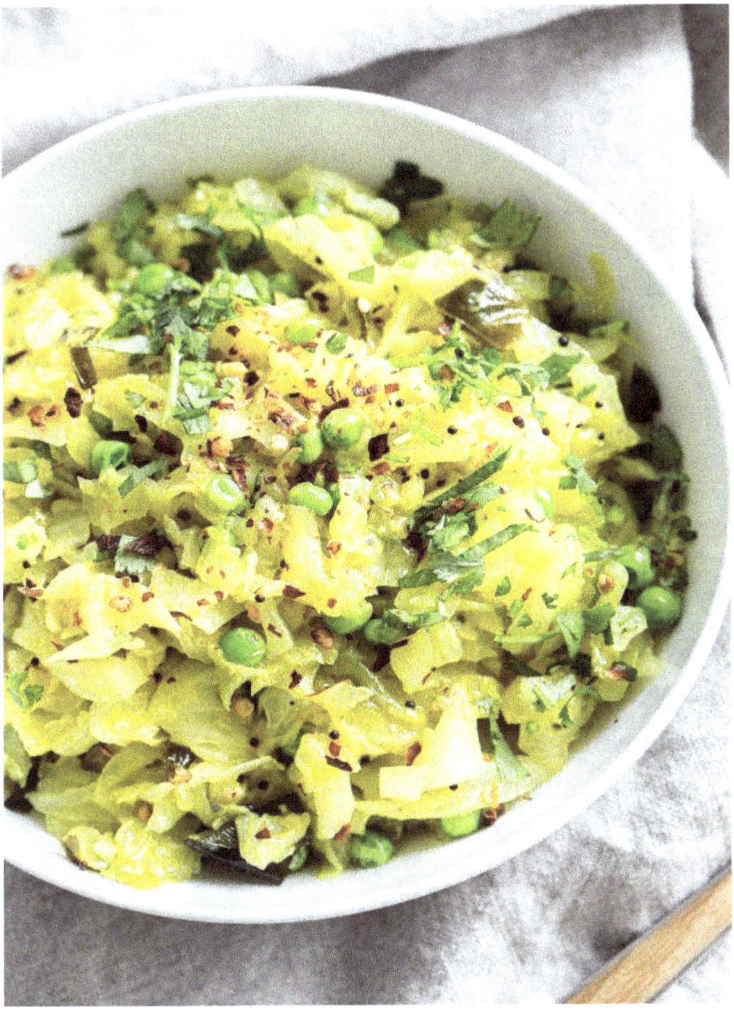

Carrot Curry

Gajjar Bhaji

- ½ cup carrots – chopped or grated
- 1 tsp oil
- ½ tsp cumin seeds
- ½ tsp ginger
- 2 pinch cinnamon
- 2 pinch black pepper
- 2 tsp fresh coconut (dried if not available)
- Salt to taste
- 5 curry leaves
- Coriander leaves

1. Heat oil, add cumin seeds, salt, ginger and curry leaves.
2. Add carrots and fry for 2 minutes.
3. Add a little water (if using carrot pieces) and remaining spices. Fry until the carrots are soft.
4. Add coriander for garnish.

Optional: add green peas (4 tsp) when adding the water.

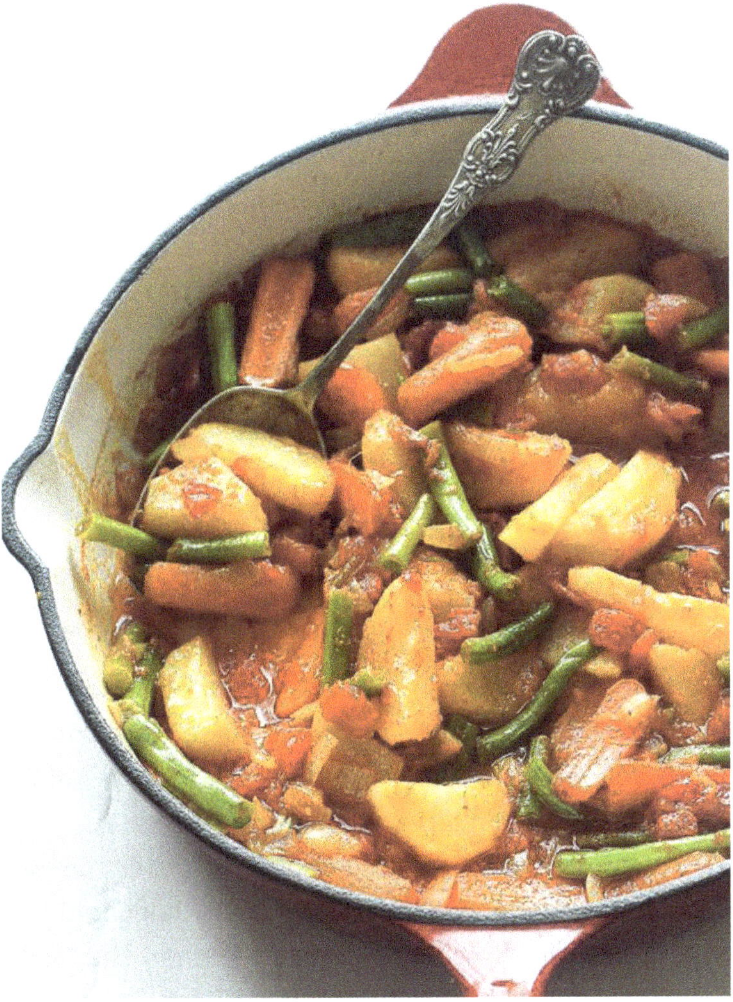

Cauliflower Curry

Phul Kobi Bhaji

- 3 cups cauliflower – cut into florets
- 2 tomatoes - chopped
- 1 tsp oil
- 1 tsp mustard seeds
- 1 tsp cumin seeds
- Pinch turmeric
- 1 tsp grated ginger
- Fresh coriander leaves
- Salt to taste
- Fresh or dried coconut - shredded

1. Heat the oil then add the mustard seeds. When they pop add the remaining spices and cook for 30 seconds. If using add the tomatoes at this point and cook for 5 minutes.
2. Add the cauliflower and a little water, cover and simmer, stirring occasionally until thoroughly cooked. If a drier curry is desired then in the last few minutes take off the lid and fry. Add coconut in the last few minutes.
3. Add salt to taste and coriander leaves.

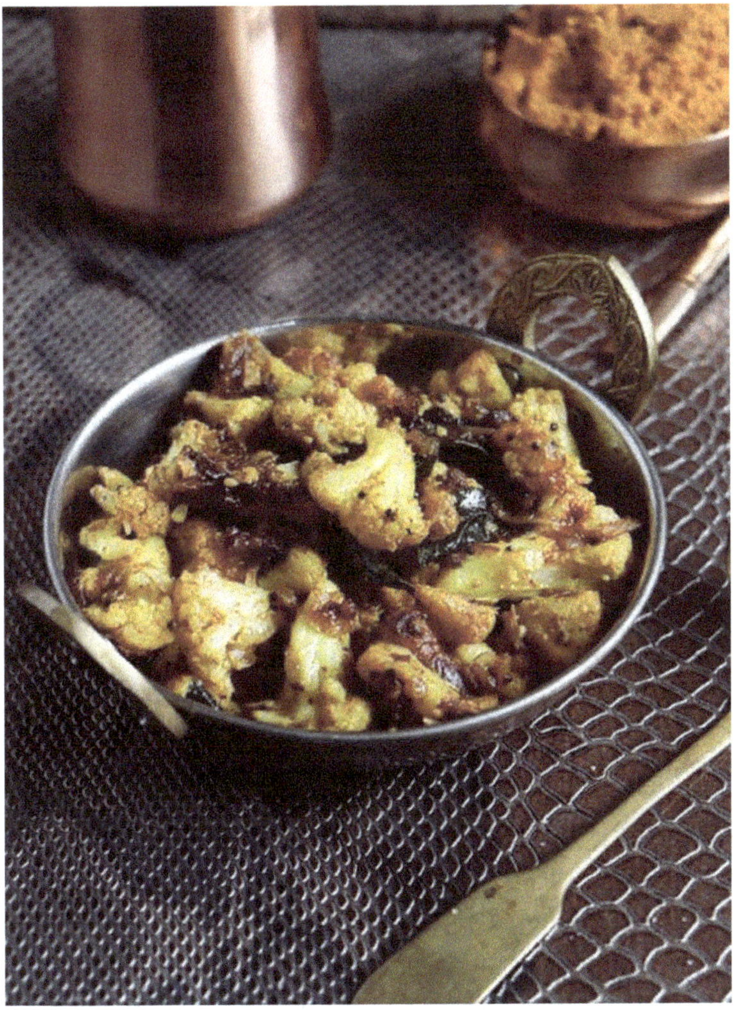

Cauliflower and Potato Curry

Phul Kobi Batata Bhaji

- 2 cups cauliflower – cut into florets
- 2 medium sized potatoes r cut in cubes
- 1 tsp oil
- 1 tsp mustard seeds
- 1 tsp cumin seeds
- 5-6 curry leaves
- Pinch turmeric - optional
- 1 tsp grated ginger
- Fresh coriander leaves
- Salt to taste
- Fresh or dried coconut – shredded
- Lemon juice – to taste

1. Heat the oil then add the mustard seeds. When they pop add the remaining spices and cook for 30 seconds.
2. Add the cauliflower and potato plus a little water, cover and simmer, stirring occasionally until almost cooked. Take off the lid and fry until the vegetables are cooked and the water has evaporated. Add coconut, salt, coriander leaves and lemon juice.

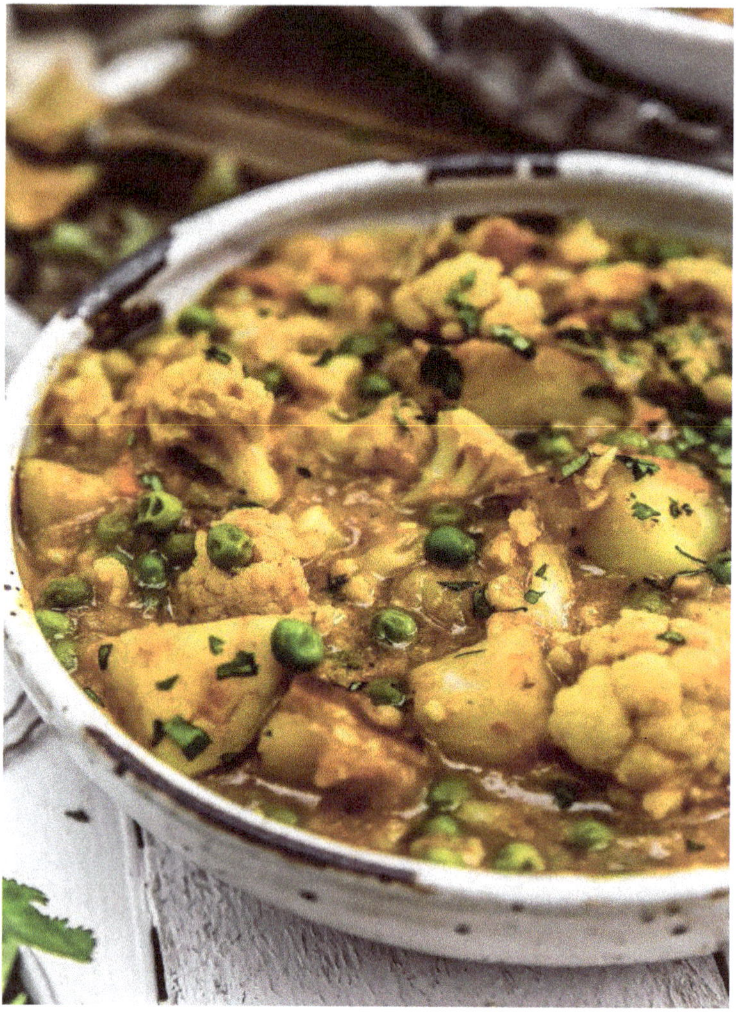

Mixed Vegetable & Lentil Curry

Sambhar

This vegetable dish usually accompanies idli or dosa. This is a famous South Indian dish.

- ¼ cup toor or mung dal
- ½ cup vegetables – sliced (carrots, potato, cauliflower, drumstick, etc.)
- 1 cup water
- 2 tsp oil
- ½ tsp cumin seeds
- ½ tsp grated ginger
- 5-6 curry leaves
- 2 tomatoes - chopped
- Lemon or tamarind to taste (or ½ - 1tsp tamarind paste)
- Jaggery to taste
- ½ salt or to taste
- Sambhar masala (see Masala section, use one load)
- Coriander leaves
- Fresh or dried coconut

1. Boil together toor dal and vegetables in a pressure cooker 15-20 minutes (1 whistle) or in a pot.
2. In a separate pan heat oil and add cumin seeds, ginger and curry leaves. Add tomatoes and cook 3-4 minutes.

3.   Add sambhar masala mixture and vegetable dal mixture.

4.   Boil together for a minute and then and add tamarind or lemon, jaggery and salt. Boil for 2-3 more minutes. Garnish with coconut and coriander

*Can add chilli if desired.

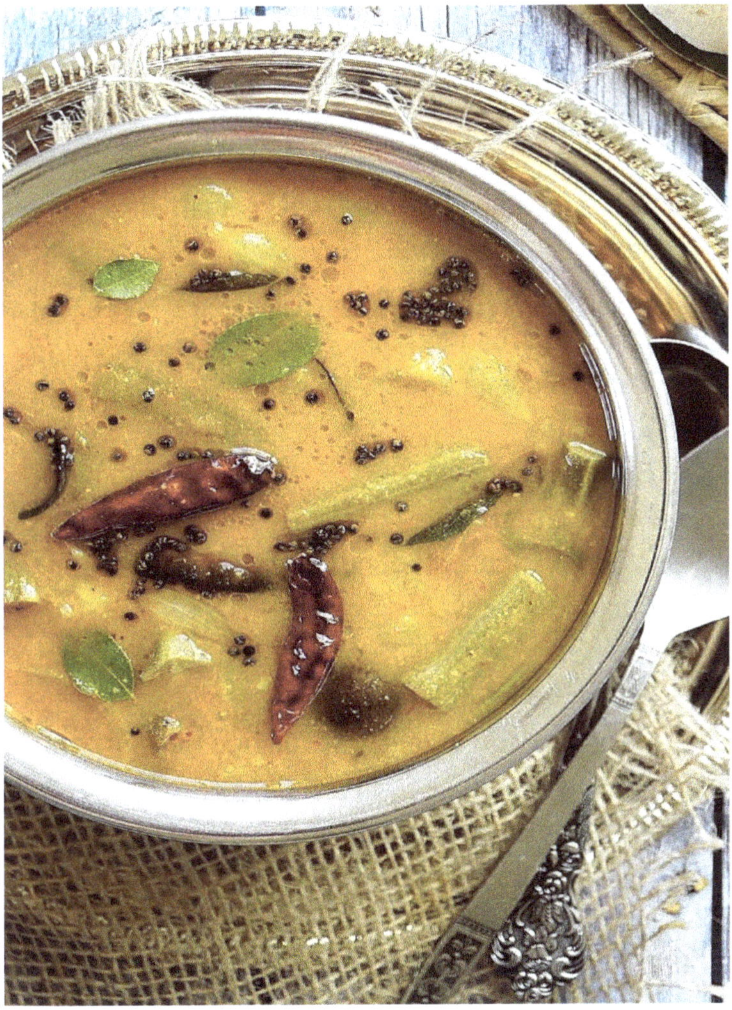

Okra / Ladies Finger Curry

Bhendi Bhaji

- 250 gms okra (ladies finger) – cut into one cm pieces
- 2 tsp grated ginger
- 1 tsp mustard seeds
- 1/2 tsp cumin seeds
- 2 tsp oil
- Salt to taste
- Pinch asafoetida
- 2-3 tsp roasted peanut powder
- Coriander leaves

1. Heat the oil and add the mustard seeds. When they pop add cumin, asafoetida and ginger. Cook for 30 seconds.
2. Add the okra and salt and stir until cooked.
3. Add the peanut powder, cook for another 30 seconds.
4. Serve with coriander leaves.

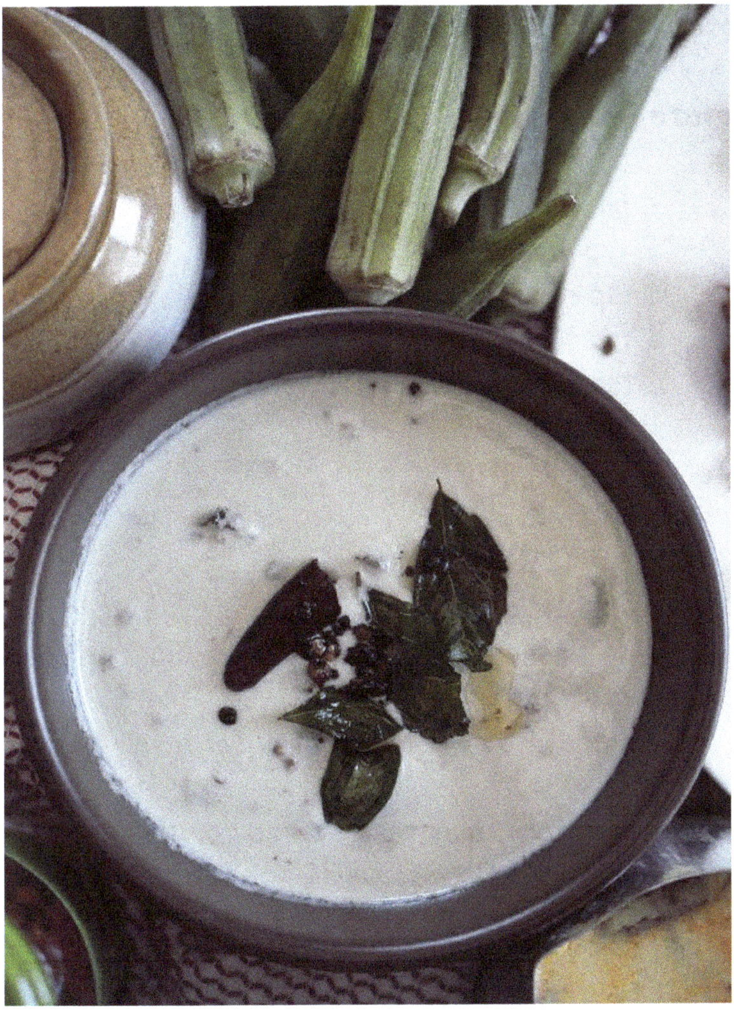

Potato Curry – Boiled

Batata Bhaji

- 4 potatoes – chopped and boiled
- 2 tsp urid dal
- 1 tsp cumin seeds
- 1 tsp turmeric
- 1 tsp grated ginger
- 5-6 curry leaves
- 2 tsp oil
- Salt to taste

1. Heat the oil, add cumin and curry leaves.
2. Add turmeric and urid dal, then ginger. Fry for 30 seconds.
3. Add potato and salt and fry for a few minutes.
4. Leave for 5 minutes covered for the flavours to blend then serve.

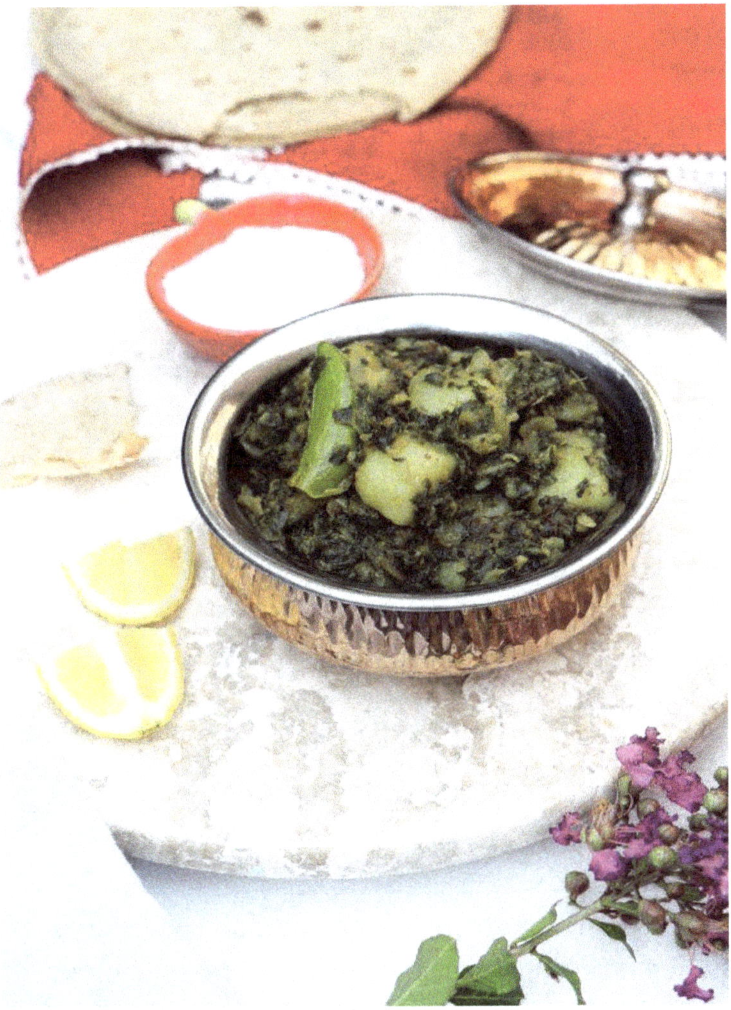

Potato Curry – Raw

Kacharya Batata Bhaji

- 4 medium sized potatoes r cut into small slices
- 1 tsp oil
- 1 tsp mustard seeds
- 1 tsp cumin seeds
- 5-6 curry leaves
- Pinch turmeric
- 1 tsp grated ginger
- ¼ cup water
- 2 tsp roasted peanut powder
- Fresh coriander leaves
- Salt to taste

1. Heat the oil then add the mustard seeds. When they pop add the remaining spices and cook for 30 seconds.
2. Add the potato, water and salt, cover and simmer, stirring occasionally until almost cooked. Take off the lid and fry until the potato is cooked and the water has evaporated. Add the peanut powder and stir for 10 seconds.
3. Add coriander leaves and serve.

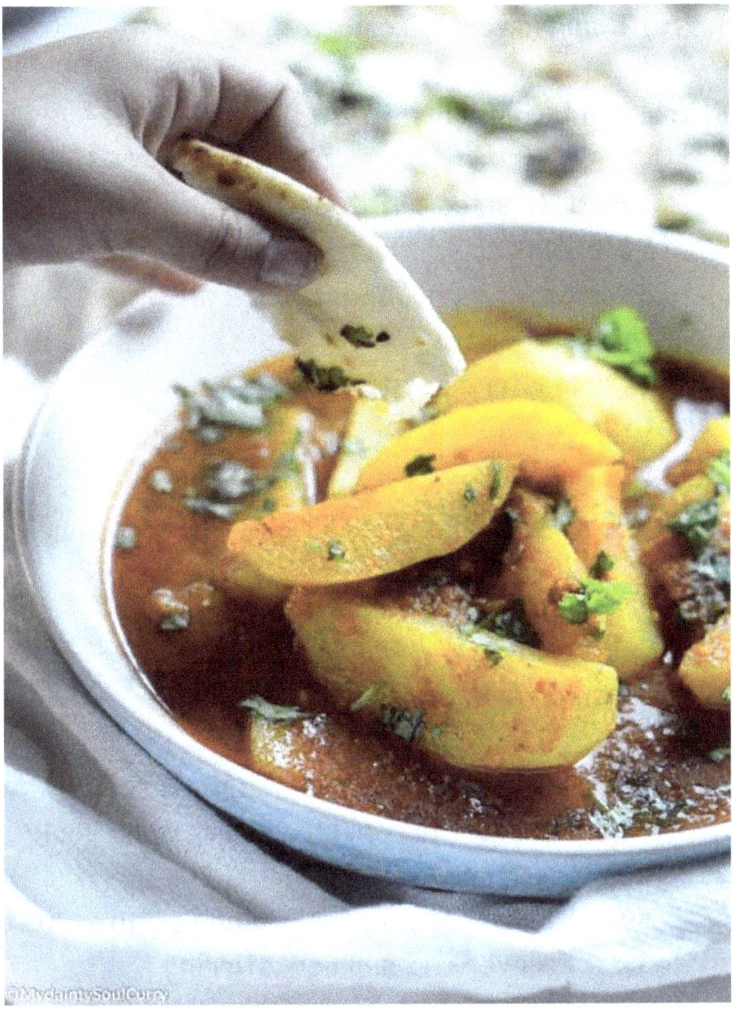

Potato, Cauliflower & Tomato Curry

Batata, Phul Kobi Tomato Bhaji

- 2 medium sized potatoes r cut in cubes
- 1 1/2 cups cauliflower - cut into florets
- 3 tomatoes r chopped in large pieces
- 1 tsp oil
- 1 tsp mustard seeds
- 1 tsp cumin seeds
- 5-6 curry leaves
- Pinch turmeric - optional
- 1 tsp grated ginger
- Fresh coriander leaves
- Salt to taste
- Fresh or dried coconut - shredded

1. Heat the oil then add the mustard seeds. When they pop add the remaining spices and cook for 30 seconds.
2. Add the cauliflower, tomato and potato plus a little water, cover and simmer, stirring occasionally until cooked. There should be some liquid remaining. If you want a dry curry then fry for a few minutes until the water has evaporated.
3. Add coconut, salt and coriander leaves.

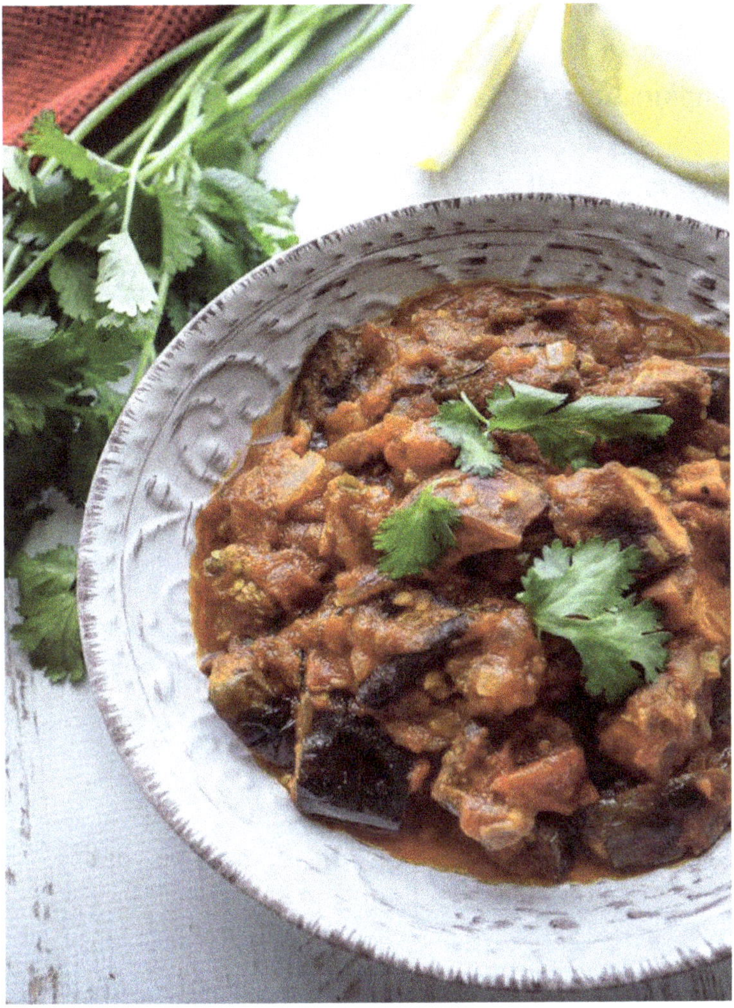

Pumpkin Curry

Lal Bopla Bhaji

- 3 cups pumpkin – chopped in 1-2 cm pieces
- 2 tsp oil
- ½ tsp mustard seeds
- ½ tsp cumin seeds
- Pinch asafoetida
- 5-6 curry leaves
- ¼ tsp fenugreek seeds
- 1/4 tsp fennel seeds
- 1/2 tsp grated ginger
- 2 inch piece dry tamarind fruit (soaked in hot water) or 1 tsp tamarind paste
- 2 Tbsp - dry, ground coconut
- 2 Tbsp roasted ground peanut
- Salt and brown sugar or jaggery to taste
- Fresh coriander leaves

1. Heat the oil and add the mustard seeds. When they pop add the cumin, fenugreek, asafoetida, ginger, curry leaves and fennel. Cook for 30 seconds.
2. Add pumpkin and salt.
3. Add the tamarind paste or water with pulp inside. Add the jaggery or brown sugar.
4. Add ground coconut and peanut powder. Cook

for a few more minutes.
5.   Add fresh chopped coriander.

Optional – you can add ½ cup sprouted beans at the time of cooking the pumpkin.

Stir Fry Vegetables

This is not an Indian dish but is a regular at the ashram.

- 3 cups chopped vegetables such as cabbage, carrot, potato, broccoli, sweet corn, green pepper, green beans, okra, tomato etc
- 2 tsp grated ginger
- 1 tsp oil
- ¼ tsp asafoetida
- 1 Tbsp (or to taste) soy sauce
- Salt and sugar to taste
- Fresh herbs – such as coriander leaves, mint leaves or basil leaves

1.   Heat the oil in a pan. Add the asafoetida and ginger. Fry for 30 seconds.
2.   Add the vegetables that need to cook the longest such as potato and carrot. Fry for a minute

and then add a little water, cover and simmer until half cooked.

3. Add the remaining vegetables such as tomato, sweet corn and green pepper. Add the soy sauce, sugar and salt. Cover and simmer till almost cooked.

4. Remove the lid and fry for a few more minutes.

5. Add the fresh herbs and leave a few minutes for the herbs to blend with the vegetables.

- Any vegetables can be used plus marinated tofu, sprouted beans and/or nuts can be added.
- Cooked rice or noodles can be added to turn it into a complete meal.

Tomato Curry

Tomato Rasa Bhaji

- 250gms tomatoes – chopped into one inch pieces or smaller if desired
- 1 tsp oil
- ½ tsp mustard seeds
- ½ tsp cumin seeds
- 4-5 curry leaves
- Pinch turmeric
- Pinch asafoetida
- 1 tsp grated ginger

- 1 potato – cooked and mashed – optional – to thicken
- 1 to 2 Tbsp roasted peanut powder
- 1 Tbsp dry coconut - optional
- Sugar and salt for taste
- Coriander leaves

1. Heat the oil and add the mustard seeds. When they pop add the cumin, curry leaves, turmeric, asafoetida and ginger. Cook for 30 seconds.
2. Add the tomato and continue stirring occasionally until cooked. Water can be added for a more liquid curry.
3. Add the roasted peanut powder, sugar, salt and coconut if using, plus the mashed potato. Cook for another minute. Serve with fresh coriander leaves.

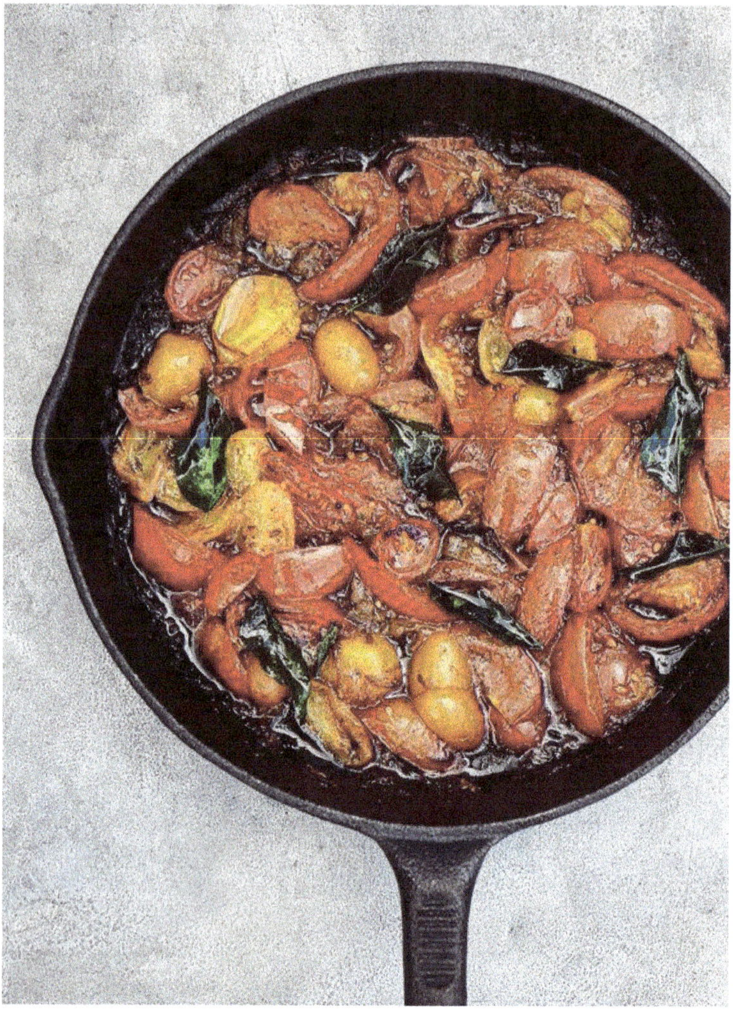

White Gourd Curry

Dudhi Bopla Bhaji

- 250 gms white gourd/white pumpkin/dudhi bopla – chopped
- 1 tsp oil
- ½ tsp mustard seeds
- ½ tsp cumin seeds
- 4-5 curry leaves
- Pinch turmeric
- Pinch asafoetida
- 1 tsp grated ginger
- 1 to 2 Tbsp roasted peanut powder
- Brown sugar and salt to taste

1. Heat the oil and add the mustard seeds. When they pop add the cumin, curry leaves, turmeric, asafoetida and ginger. Cook for 30 seconds.
2. Add the white pumpkin, a little water, cover and simmer, stirring occasionally until cooked.
3. Add the roasted peanut powder, sugar and salt and cook for another minute.

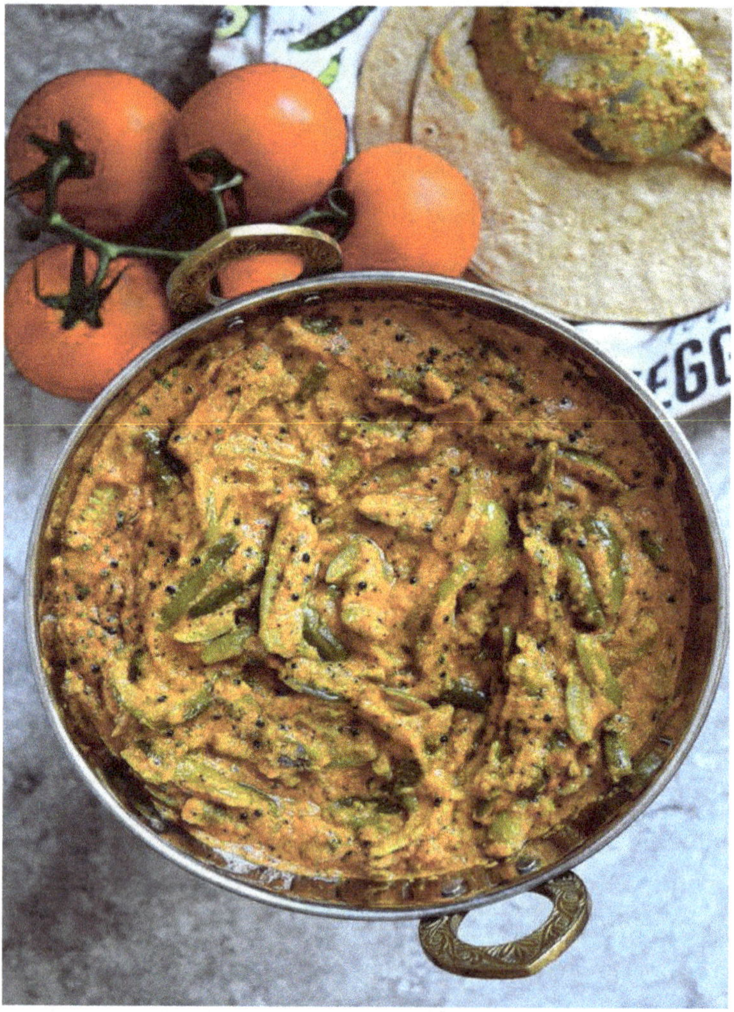

CPSIA information can be obtained
at www.ICGtesting.com
Printed in the USA
BVHW091007280421
606021BV00002B/80

9 781801 977555